Pressure Cooker, Dump Dinners Cookbook, Clean Eating Diet and My Spiralized Cookbook Box Set:

Over 100 Delicious And Healthy Recipes For You And Your Family

by Eric Deen

Published in United States by:

Eric Deen

© Copyright 2015 – Eric Deen

ISBN-13: 978-1516992416
ISBN-10: 1516992415

Table of Contents

Book 1
Pressure Cooker: 30+ Delicious and Quick Pressure Cooker Recipes for You and Your Family

Introduction

Ready to learn the most delicious and quick Pressure Cooker recipes to share with your family and friends?

You are really going to enjoy trying out this great collection of pressure cooker recipes. Included in this book is a bonus collection of desert recipes that I am sure you and your loved ones will enjoy! It is always a good idea to find new ways to keep your mind stimulated, and this certainly includes learning new ways to prepare your foods.

Using a pressure cooker to prepare your foods is an amazing method that everyone should try. It is unlike any other way that you have prepared your meals in the past. Using a pressure cooker is a form of cooking that is in a class of its own. It may seem a bit strange to you at first as you will have to get used to the fact that it is sealed so that you cannot take the lid on and off throughout the cooking of the food.

Also keep in mind the top six benefits to pressure cooking your food:

1. Your food will retain most of its nutrients making them tastier.

2. Saves time when it comes to preparing meals, cook time is greatly reduced.

3. It is a great energy saver, it is much more efficient that having multiple pots on separate burners. Pressure cookers tend to offer more of one-pot cooking recipes in general.

4. It keeps your kitchen cooler, a pressure cooker retains the heat and steam resulting in a cooler kitchen.

5. Less cleaning is involved with a pressure cooker, you won't have the spray that you get from other pots and pans messing up the surrounding areas. The pressure cooker is a secured pot that prevents spatters and splashes from occurring.

6. You can also use your pressure cooker to preserve food so that you can use them at a later date by canning foods. You can get larger models to use for holding more

jars the larger models are referred to as "canners."

I am sure like most people you are used to taking the lid of your pot and tasting your special meal you are preparing during the cooking process. You will be learning a whole new approach that this step is not included. Learning the art of proper pressure cooking requires a certain amount of knowledge that the average person does not have. But you are all set to pressure cook your way into some tasty meals to serve to your loved ones, you are now armed with this easy to follow pressure cooker cookbook.

Following the instructions in this cookbook you will be able to make some great dishes that will have your loved wants asking for seconds. You will find that preparing meals with your pressure cooker will give you time to do other things besides standing over a hot stove for two or three hours. You will be able to leave the pressure cooker and let it take care of cooking the meal while you are able to perhaps spend time with you loved ones.

The recipes that are in this book are not only great tasting, but they are also quick and easy to prepare. You will be able to take inexpensive cuts of meat and by cooking them in your pressure cooker you will make them taste so yummy and tender. You will have the freedom to get other things done while the pressure cooker cooks the meal or just sit down and relax for a while.

Use the recipes in this cookbook as a base, don't be afraid to add things that you enjoy into the recipe. Make it your own by adding your own special ingredients to the recipe. This is how you can build some wonderful recipes that you and your loved ones can enjoy over a lifetime. When your children are grown they can take their favorite pressure cooker recipes with them. Perhaps as a house warming gift you can get them their own pressure cooker when they leave home. But for now we will stick to the present and make some great pressure cooker meals for you and your loved ones using this cookbook to guide you through a new level in the cooking experience that you are sure to love! Now it is time to open these pages and choose the first recipe that you will make using your pressure cooker—the beginning of many tasty meals to come!

Chapter 1:
Mixture of Pressure Cooker Recipes 1-5

1. Pork Roast

Total Time Needed: one hour

Ingredients:

- three pounds of pork loin, boneless
- half a teaspoon of dry mustard
- half a teaspoon of sage
- half a teaspoon of sea salt
- two teaspoons of paprika
- two cups of Leeks, chopped
- one teaspoon of coconut oil

- one teaspoon of parsley, dried
- one teaspoon of garlic, minced
- two cups of chicken broth
- two cups of water
- one teaspoon of ground black pepper
- one red onion, minced
- half a teaspoon of thyme

Directions:

Add oil to the bottom of cooker and allow to heat on high. Add pork roast to the heated oil and allow to brown on all sides. Set aside and allow to cool. Add garlic, leeks, onions and cook for five minutes until soft. Pour your water and broth in and allow to heat. In a bowl mix spices together, mustard, thyme, pepper, sage, paprika, parsley. Rub roast with spice mix, then place into liquid in your cooker. Secure the lid and allow the cooker to rise to high pressure. Once it is at high pressure cook for 45 minutes. Release the lid to cool the pressure cooker, and serve.

2. Pressure Cooker Whole Chicken

Total Time Needed: 30 minutes

Ingredients:

- two pound whole chicken
- pepper and salt to taste
- two tablespoons of coconut oil
- one and a half cups of chicken broth
- one teaspoon of poultry seasoning

Directions:

Rinse the chicken then use hand towels to pat it dry. Mix seasoning—pepper, salt, and poultry seasoning in bowl, then add to chicken. Set your oil to heat in the pressure cooker when it is hot brown the season on all sides then set aside. Put a food rack inside your pressure cooker, place chicken on top. Pour broth around the chicken the secure lid of pressure cooker. Once the pressure cooker has raised to high pressure allow to cook for 25 minutes. Remove the cooker from the flame and allow it to cool under running water to release the lid. Carve up the chicken and enjoy with a favorite side dish.

3. Pressure Cooked Artichokes

Total Time Needed: 20 minutes

Ingredients:

- eight baby artichokes
- two tablespoons of coconut oil
- one lemon
- four cloves of garlic, diced

Directions:

Trim the tops of your artichokes. Dice the garlic cloves and put the pieces in between the artichoke leaves. Then place them into a steamer basket in your pressure cooker. Add a slice of lemon with the artichokes in the cooker. Drizzle with melted coconut oil. Secure the lid and allow it to rise to high pressure. Once it is at high pressure cook for 12 minutes. Cool the cooker by running under cool water. Garnish artichokes with lemon slices and serve.

4. Pressure Cooked Hard Boiled Eggs

Total Time Needed: 15 minutes

Ingredients:

- two cups of water
- eight eggs

Directions:

Pour the water into your pressure cooker, place steamer tray into cooker and place your eggs on the steamer tray, make sure basket is above water. Secure the lid and allow to rise to low pressure. Once at that point allow eggs to cook for six minutes. Remove pressure cooker from heat and let stand for five minutes. Cool pressure cooker under cold running water, carefully open the lid. Peel the eggs and serve.

5. Ham & Navy Bean Soup

Total Time Needed: 40 minutes

Ingredients:

- one quarter cup of minced green pepper
- four pieces of celery, sliced
- four carrots, sliced
- two teaspoons of sea salt
- half a cup of coconut oil, melted
- four cups of dried navy beans, pre-soaked
- three pounds of ham shanks
- two cups of tomato sauce
- one teaspoon of garlic, minced
- pepper to taste
- three quarts of water

Directions:

Discard the liquid that you were soaking the beans in. Pour all of your ingredients into the pressure cooker and secure the lid. Cook for 30 minutes on high pressure. Allow the pressure cooker to cool down on its own. Serve and enjoy this yummy soup!

Chapter 2- Mixture of Pressure Cooker Recipes 6-10

6. Caribbean Oxtail & Beans

Total Time Needed: 1 1/4 hours

Ingredients:

- one large onion, chopped
- one pound of oxtail, chopped
- one green onion, thinly sliced
- one teaspoon of ginger root, fresh
- one sprig of thyme, chopped
- two tablespoons of soy sauce
- one Scotch Bonnet pepper, chopped

- half a teaspoon of sea salt
- one teaspoon of ground black pepper
- two tablespoons of coconut oil, melted
- one and a half cups of water and another separate two tablespoons of water
- one cup of Fava beans, drained
- one teaspoon of allspice berries
- one tablespoon of cornstarch

Directions:

In a large mixing bowl combine your green onion garlic, thyme, ginger, soy sauce, pepper, and oxtail. Toss and massage oxtail. In a large skillet heat the oil and brown the oxtail pieces on all sides over a medium high heat. Put into the pressure cooker once browned. Add water. Secure the lid and allow it to rise to high pressure. Once at high pressure allow it to cook for 25 minutes. Remove the cooker from heat and allow to cool naturally then remove the lid carefully. Put in the beans and allspice. Create a slurry with two tablespoons of water and cornstarch. Mix this into the pressure cooker and stir well.

7. Pressure Cooker Barbeque Chicken

Total Time Needed: 45 minutes

Ingredients:
- three chicken breast halves with bone
- two teaspoons of chicken bouillon
- one twelve ounce can of beer
- half a cup of water
- one teaspoon of Nutmeg
- one teaspoon of Cinnamon
- half a teaspoon of Ginger
- two teaspoons of salt
- one eighth teaspoon of fresh ground pepper
- barbeque sauce of your choosing

Directions:
Add ginger, nutmeg, cinnamon, salt, and pepper into a container. Put the chicken into the container and massage. Proceed to pour your water, beer, and chicken bouillon into the pressure cooker. Add your seasoned chicken to the liquid in the pressure cooker and allow to rise to high pressure over a high flame. Cook at high pressure for 20 minutes. Allow the cooker to cool down naturally then grill for 10 minutes. Brush on barbeque sauce and grill for another five minutes and enjoy!

8. Pressure Cooker Potato Salad

Total Time Needed: One and a half hours

Ingredients:
- one stalk of celery, chopped
- one quarter cup of red onion, chopped
- one cup of water
- six red potatoes, scrubbed, and chopped
- one teaspoon of apple cider vinegar
- one teaspoon of Dijon Mustard
- half a cup of Mayonnaise
- one tablespoon of dill, fresh, chopped
- three hard-boiled eggs, chopped
- salt and pepper to taste
- half a cup of sweet pickles, finely diced

Directions:
Pour water and potatoes into your pressure cooker. Securely close the lid and allow to rise to high pressure over a high flame. Cook for about five minutes. Remove the cooker from the flame and cool under cold running water. Peel and dice potatoes, layer them with celery, and onion. Season with salt and pepper, add dill, and chopped eggs. In a separate bowl combine vinegar, pickles, mustard, and mayonnaise. Fold this mixture gently into the potatoes. Chill for at least one hour.

9. Pressure Cooker Quinoa

Total Time Needed: 15 minutes

Ingredients:

- two cups of whole grain quinoa
- two tablespoons of coconut oil, melted
- one teaspoon of garlic, minced
- two teaspoons of Turmeric
- three cups of water
- one teaspoon of sea salt
- two teaspoons of Cumin
- Herbs, fresh to garnish

Directions:

Empty quinoa into a fine mesh strainer and rinse under running water, rub the grains in the strainer. Preheat your pressure cooker over medium heat, pour in oil, add garlic, and saute until soft. Mix in your cumin, turmeric, and salt. Pour in your water then add the quinoa. Securely close lid, allow to rise to high pressure, heat over low flame for a minute. Allow to cool naturally and then open and tumble and fluff quinoa and serve.

10. Spicy Ribs

Total Time Needed: 30 minutes

Ingredients:

- one tablespoon of brown sugar
- four tablespoons of red wine
- two tablespoons of Worcestershire sauce
- three cups of ketchup
- one tablespoon of almond flour
- one cup of water
- one large onion, chopped
- one teaspoon of Dijon Mustard
- two teaspoons of chili powder
- one teaspoon of sea salt
- one teaspoon of black ground pepper
- two tablespoons of coconut oil
- one teaspoon of garlic, minced

Directions:

In a bowl mix ingredients except for ribs, oil, onion, water, and flour. Add ribs to mix and stir thoroughly, and marinate in fridge for four hours. Divide the ribs into two portions and save the marinade for later. Heat the oil in the fast cooker for about two minutes; fry the beef in batches from all sides. With the remaining oil after frying, add onions, and then fry until they brown. Add ribs, marinade, one cup of water, and mix. Close the pressure cooker, bring to a full power using high heat. Reduce the heat and cook for 30 minutes. Remove them from heat and put them aside to cool. Open the pressure cooker, arrange ribs on plates, and remove grease from cooker. In a separate bowl, gradually add the one cup of water to flour, while stirring the flour constantly with remaining fluid in pressure cooker, whisk constantly. Put the pressure cooker on medium heat and cook the sauce for three minutes, keep stirring as it cooks. Pour the sauce over the ribs and serve warm.

Chapter 3:
Chapter 3- Mixture of Pressure Cooker Recipes 11-15

11. Chow Mein

Total Time Needed: 25 minutes

Ingredients:

- one teaspoon of garlic, minced
- two teaspoons of almond flour
- two eggs
- two ounces of mushrooms, sliced
- seven ounces of cabbage, sliced

- two stalks of celery, cut into slices
- seven ounces of chicken breast, boned, and skinned
- salt to taste
- seven tablespoons of peanut oil
- two teaspoons of apple cider vinegar
- two teaspoons of tomato sauce
- two teaspoons of chili sauce
- two teaspoons of soy sauce
- one inch of ginger piece, cut into slices
- seven ounces of noodles
- one leek, trimmed, and sliced
- half a cup of chicken broth

Directions:

Rinse chicken then cook in the pressure cooker with half a cup of water for ten minutes. Save the broth and cut the chicken into strips. Pour three cups of water into pot, add noodles, and salt. Close the pressure cooker and bring it to full power on high heat. Reduce the heat to medium and cook for five minutes. Remove from heat then open pressure cooker to remove built up steam. Pour cold water over pasta in strainer, leave to cool. In a skillet, heat one tablespoon of oil, pour lightly beaten eggs, and stir-fry until dense. Cut the omelet into strips and remove from pan. Now heat two tablespoons of oil in same pan and saute garlic, leeks, cabbage, mushrooms, ginger, and chicken. Add half a cup of chicken broth mixed with soy sauce and almond flour. Simmer until it thickens. Add tomato sauce, chili sauce, and vinegar. In a different pan, heat cooked noodles with remaining oil. Transfer to a platter and garnish with strips of omelet; pour over the sauce, chicken, and vegetables, serve hot.

12. Spring Meatballs

Total Time Needed: 12 minutes

Ingredients:

- one pound of lean ground beef
- half a pound of ground pork
- one teaspoon of grated lemon peel
- one teaspoon of paprika
- one teaspoon of salt
- one small onion, finely chopped
- two eggs
- two slices of whole wheat bread soaked in water, and squeezed
- two tablespoons of chive
- six tablespoons of almond flour
- six tablespoons of butter
- three cups of natural vegetable broth
- five tablespoons of parsley, chopped
- four teaspoons of freshly squeezed lemon juice

Directions:

In a bowl mix all the ingredients except for half of the lemon juice, butter, broth, chives, and flour. Divide the mixture to 24 portions and form balls of about 4 centimeters in diameter. Pour the broth into the pressure cooker, bring it to a boil over high heat, and add the meatballs one by one. Close the pressure cooker and bring to full power over high heat. Reduce heat and cook for four minutes. Remove the pressure cooker from the heat and allow to cool slowly. Open the pressure cooker, place meatballs on plates, and keep warm. Strain the remaining liquid after cooking and save it for later. Melt the butter in the pressure cooker over medium heat. Add flour and cook over low heat, stirring constantly for about four minutes. Remove from heat and gradually add the preserved liquid to it. Put the pressure cooker on medium heat. Boil and stir constantly until the sauce thickens. Add the remaining lemon juice, and parsley. Serve with warm pasta or rice.

13. Spicy Italian Chicken & Sausage

Total Time Needed: 40

Ingredients:

- two red peppers, sliced
- one onion, diced
- two chicken breasts, sliced, skinless, and boneless
- four Italian sausages
- one tablespoon of coconut oil
- one teaspoon of garlic, minced
- two tablespoons of red wine vinegar
- 16 ounces of tomatoes, diced
- salt and pepper to taste
- red pepper flakes
- one quarter teaspoon of Fennel seeds
- three quarter teaspoon of Basil

Directions:

Heat your oil in your pressure cooker. While oil is heating skin your sausages. Add chicken and sausages to hot oil brown on all sides. Dice onion, slice peppers. Remove browned meat from the cooker. Add vegetables to heated cooker, allow them to cook until they have become soft. Add vinegar and stir. Add chicken, sausage, tomatoes, fennel, basil, red pepper, salt and pepper.

Secure the lid on the pressure cooker allow to rise to high pressure. Once at high pressure reduce the heat so pressure will stabilize and cook for another ten minutes. Allow the cooker to cool, open lid, and serve.

14. Ribs, Beer & Honey

Total Time Needed: 25 minutes

Ingredients:

- two pounds of ribs
- two tablespoons of coconut oil
- one cup of organic honey
- one cup of non-alcoholic beer
- one teaspoon of Dijon mustard
- one teaspoon of chili powder
- one teaspoon of lemon juice, fresh squeezed
- one teaspoon of sage
- two teaspoons of sea salt

Directions:

Divide the ribs into three parts. Heat your oil in the pressure cooker for two minutes, fry ribs in batches on all sides. Remove the pressure cooker from heat and remove grease. Add the ribs and the rest of the ingredients while stirring. Close the pressure cooker and bring to its full power over high heat. Reduce to medium heat and cook for twenty minutes. Remove the pressure cooker from heat and leave to cool slowly. Open the pressure cooker arrange the ribs on serving dishes, and keep them warm. Remove grease from liquid that remained after cooking.

Put pressure cooker on medium heat and cook until the sauce's volume is reduced by half then pour over ribs and serve.

15. Cooked Beef with Dumplings

Total Time Needed: 20 minutes

Ingredients:

* one pound of beef loin, cut into cubes, two inches in size
* salt and pepper to taste
* one bay leaf
* two large onions, sliced
* two large carrots, sliced into strips
* half a cup of beef broth

Dumplings:

* a pinch of baking powder
* four ounces of almond flour
* one medium onion chopped
* one tablespoon of parsley, chopped
* salt and pepper to taste

Directions:

Dumplings: Mix all of the ingredients, add some water, and knead as dough. Form twelve small balls. Boil six fluid ounces of water in pressure cooker and add the dumplings. Close the pressure cooker and bring to its full power over high heat. Reduce the heat to a minimum and cook for eight minutes. Open immediately after the release of the steam. Remove dumplings from the pot.

Beef: Pour half a cup of beef broth in the pressure cooker. Add beef, onion, bay leaf, salt and pepper. Close the pressure cooker and bring to its full power over high heat. Reduce heat to a medium heat and cook for 15 minutes. Leave the pressure cooker to cool slowly. Once cooled open and add carrots. Close the pressure cooker and bring to its full power over high heat. Reduce heat to minimum and cook for three minutes. Once again leave the pressure cooker to cool slowly before opening. Serve warm with dumplings.

Chapter 4:
Chapter 4- Pressure Cooker Fish Recipes 16-20

16. Pressure Cooker Fish Fillets

Total Time Needed: 10 minutes

Ingredients:

- three cups of mushrooms, thinly sliced
- 6 sole fillets
- two tablespoons of lemon juice
- salt and pepper to taste
- three tablespoons of organic butter
- half of small red onion, finely chopped
- two cloves garlic, finely chopped
- one cup of celery, finely chopped

- three cups of water
- one teaspoon of thyme, ground
- one handful of dill, fresh
- four green olives, pitted, and sliced
- one large tomato, peeled, and sliced
- one cup of dry white wine

Directions:

Rub the fish with lemon juice, pepper, and salt, marinate for one hour. Melt butter in a saucepan, add garlic, onion, and celery. Stir-fry until onion is slightly browned. Add mushrooms and wine; cook until the wine evaporates. Add tomato, olives, dill and some salt. Cook until the fluid has evaporated. Place each fillet on a piece of aluminum foil. Evenly spread the mixture over fish and wrap foil around the fish. Fold the top and sides to form packets. Pour water into the pressure cooker and put rack or inset into cooker. Place the fish packets on top of inset. Close the pressure cooker and bring to full pressure on high heat. Reduce the heat and cook for three minutes. Remove the pressure cooker from heat and release the steam. Open the pressure cooker and arrange the fish on to serving plates and enjoy!

17. Sweet & Sour Shrimps

Total Time Needed: 10 minutes

Ingredients:

- one stalk of celery, cut into diagonal strips
- eight ounces of shrimp, deveined, and cleaned
- four ounces of cucumber, cut into diagonal strips
- three yellow peppers, cut into strips
- two medium carrots, cut into diagonal strips
- one leek, cut into diagonal strips
- two cups of peanut oil
- salt to taste

Sauce:

- one teaspoon of sugar
- two tablespoons of cornstarch
- two tablespoons of tomato sauce
- four teaspoons of soy sauce
- four teaspoons of organic honey
- one cup of apple cider vinegar

Dough:

- two tablespoons of almond flour

- one teaspoon of baking powder
- two eggs
- one cup of milk

Directions:

In the pressure cooker and a cup of water and add the cleaned shrimp. Close the pressure cooker and bring to full boil on high heat. Reduce the heat to medium and cook for five minutes. Remove the pressure cooker from heat and open to allow steam to be released. Remove the shrimps and drain. Prepare the dough, beat eggs, add flour, and milk. Finally add salt, and baking powder. Add it bit of water to get it like batter-like dough. In a pan heat oil, dip shrimps in batter and fry until golden and crispy. Remove the shrimp and stir-fry the vegetables, drying them on paper towel. In a skillet mix flour, salt, sugar, vinegar, honey, soy sauce, and tomato sauce. Add the vegetables and shrimp; bring to boil and heat for four minutes, then enjoy.

18. Fish Steak & Mushrooms

Total Time Needed: 10 minutes

Ingredients:

- one inch piece of ginger, freshly grated
- one tablespoon of sugar
- one teaspoon of sea salt
- two large pieces of halibut steaks, two centimeters thick
- one cup of mushrooms, thinly sliced
- one cup of shallots, with chives, chopped
- save one tablespoon of chives for garnish
- three tablespoons of soy sauce
- one cup of dry white wine
- one tablespoon of white wine vinegar

Directions:

In a shallow bowl, mix all ingredients except fish, mushrooms, and shallots. Add fish steaks, dip them in the sauce, and marinate for one hour. Place the insert into the cooker and place fish on top of it. Pour the marinade into the cooker, place the mushrooms, and onions on top of fish. Close the pressure cooker and bring to full pressure on high heat. Reduce heat and cook for five minutes. Remove from heat and release steam. Open the pressure cooker and arrange fish and vegetables on a serving platter. Remove the inset from pressure cooker. Place the pressure cooker over high heat and cook until the liquid is reduced to half. Stir occasionally then pour over fish and serve warm. Garnish with shallots and chives.

19. Fish Broth

Total Time Needed: 15 minutes

Ingredients:
- half a cup of celery, chopped
- one small carrot, chopped
- one small onion, chopped
- two tablespoons of organic butter
- one bay leaf
- one sprig of parsley
- pinch of white pepper
- one teaspoon of sea salt
- one teaspoon of thyme, dried
- 24 ounces of fish fillets, white non-greasy fish, with bones removed
- six pieces of asparagus, trimmed, and halved.

Directions:

Melt the butter in pressure cooker. Add onion, carrots, celery, and asparagus. Stir-fry until onion gets glossy. Add remaining ingredients and mix. Close the pressure cooker and bring to its full pressure over high heat. Reduce heat and cook for 15 minutes. Remove the pressure cooker from heat and leave to slowly cool. Open the pressure cooker and strain the broth through a fine sieve.

20. Salmon Steaks

Total Time Needed: 10 minutes

Ingredients:

- two twenty-eight ounce salmon steaks, about one inch thick
- one medium onion, sliced into rings
- one lemon, sliced
- one eighth teaspoon of pepper
- one teaspoon of sea salt
- one cup of dry white wine
- tablespoon of dill, fresh, chopped

Directions:

Put the inset into the pressure cooker and arrange the onion on it. Place the fish on the onion and drizzle with white wine. Season with salt and pepper, arrange lemon slices on the fish, save four slices to garnish serving plates. Close the pressure cooker and bring to full pressure on high heat. Reduce the heat and cook for six minutes. Remove the pressure cooker from heat and release the steam. Open the pressure cooker arrange fish on serving plates and remove the onion, and lemon. Serve warm with lemon slices on top and sprinkled with fresh dill.

Chapter 5:
Chapter 5- Pressure Cooker Poultry Recipes 21-25

21. Turkey & Lentil

Total Time Needed: 5 minutes

Ingredients:

- one cup of brown rice
- half a cup of red lentils, Egyptian don't need to be soaked
- half a red pepper, sliced
- half a green pepper, sliced
- 18 ounce turkey thigh, rinsed, drained, cut into strips
- one onion, chopped
- half of a leek, cut into long strips

- one stalk of celery, chopped
- half a cup of mushrooms, thinly sliced
- a couple of leaves of savoy cabbage
- two and a half cups of chicken broth
- one bay leaf
- sea salt, pepper, and paprika to taste
- Bechamel-cheese sauce
- four tablespoons of olive oil
- one tablespoon or so of almond flour

Directions:

Season the turkey strip and gently sprinkle with flour and saute in oil that is preheated in pressure cooker. Add onions, and continue to fry. Add rice and lentils as well as other remaining ingredients. Then pour in chicken broth. Close the pressure cooker and bring to boil. Reduce heat and cook for another three minutes. Then serve and enjoy!

22. Braised Duck

Total Time Needed: 15 minutes

Ingredients:

- thirty five ounce duck, with bones, removed, and sliced
- one lemon
- one ounce of organic butter
- five ounces of vegetable bouillon
- one tablespoon of rosemary
- ten fluid ounces of Worcestershire sauce

Directions:

In the pressure cooker melt your butter and saute the duck until browned on all sides. Add Worcestershire sauce, seasonings, and broth. Close the pressure cooker and bring to full power boiling over high heat. Reduce heat to medium and cook for 15 minutes. Leave the pressure cooker to cool slowly. Open and serve with slices of fresh lemon.

23. Chicken in Lemon Sauce

Total Time Needed: 15 minutes

Ingredients:

- three pounds of skinless chicken
- one large onion, chopped
- two tablespoons of butter
- four cups of chicken broth
- one teaspoon of thyme, dried
- one teaspoon of pepper
- two teaspoons of sea salt
- one cup of celery, chopped
- three tablespoons of lemon juice
- one tablespoon of grated lemon peel
- four tablespoons of almond flour
- one tablespoon of parsley, freshly chopped
- one lemon, sliced

Directions:

Rub chicken with two tablespoons of lemon juice then set aside for one hour. Put the chicken and remaining lemon juice into pressure cooker. Add other ingredients except for butter, flour and parsley. Mix well. Close the pressure cooker and bring to full power over high heat. Reduce the heat to medium and cook for eight minutes. Remove the pressure cooker from heat and leave to cool slowly. Open the pressure cooker; put chicken on a plate, keep warm. Strain the liquid, strain the fat and keep the liquid. Melt butter in pressure cooker on medium heat. Add flour and cook over low heat while whisking. Remove from heat and keep stirring, gradually add preserved liquid throw in lemon slices and mix. Put pressure cooker on medium heat. Cook for about four minutes until the sauce thickens. Pour sauce over chicken garnish with parsley and serve.

24. French Style Chicken in Wine Sauce

Total Time Needed: 15 minutes

Ingredients:

- one cup plus three tablespoons of almond flour
- five tablespoons of butter
- two pounds of chicken, sliced
- three ounces of ham, cut into parts or two inch cubes
- two cloves
- six shallots, peeled
- black pepper to taste
- one teaspoon of sea salt
- two tablespoons of water
- one teaspoon of garlic, minced
- one cup of chicken broth
- one cup of Burgundy wine
- three cups of mushrooms, finely chopped
- one bay leaf
- one teaspoon of thyme, dried
- one cup of Cognac
- one tablespoon of parsley, fresh, chopped

Directions:
Add one cup of flour to a plastic bag. Throw a few

pieces of chicken into bag and shake to coat with flour. Melt one tablespoon of butter in the pressure cooker. Add ham and fry until it is slightly browned. Remove from the pressure cooker and set aside. Divide the chicken into three parts- melt two tablespoons of butter in pressure cooker, fry chicken in it in three batches. Remove from pressure cooker remove from heat and rinse cooker to remove residue after cooking. Add chicken and ham back into pressure cooker.

Put pressure cooker on medium heat; add the remaining ingredients except Cognac, parsley, and remaining two tablespoons of butter and flour (3 tablespoons). Stir thoroughly. Close the pressure cooker and bring to its full power over high heat. Reduce heat to medium and cook for eight minutes. Remove the pressure cooker from heat and allow to cool slowly. Open the pressure cooker and arrange chicken on a plate keep warm. From the liquid that remained after cooking, remove the fat, and save one cup. Melt butter in pressure cooker on medium heat. Add the remaining flour on low heat stirring with a whisk for about four minutes. Remove from heat and while still stirring gradually add saved liquid. Put pressure cooker over medium heat. Continue to stir until sauce thickens. Heat Cognac in a saucepan. Set it on fire; pour the burning Cognac into the sauce. Stir and pour sauce over chicken and serve warm.

25. Ginger Chicken

Total Time Needed: 12 minutes

Ingredients:

- half of a chicken cut into two portions
- one inch of ginger, freshly grated
- one teaspoon of garlic, minced
- one shallot with chives, peeled and sliced
- one lemon, cut into thin slices
- two teaspoons of black pepper
- one teaspoon of sea salt
- one cup of water
- one cup of dry Sherry
- one cup of soy sauce
- sesame seeds for garnish

Directions:

Rub the chicken with the garlic and ginger. Pour soy sauce, water, and Sherry into the pressure cooker, then put in the inset. Put the chicken on the inset and sprinkle with salt and pepper. Place the onion and lemon slices on the chicken. Close the pressure cooker and bring it to its full power over high heat. Reduce the heat to medium and cook for an additional 10 minutes. Remove the pressure cooker from the heat and leave to cool slowly.

Open the pressure cooker and take out the chicken and set aside. Remove the insert and continue to cook sauce adding shallots, stirring for a few minutes. Then add chicken back into pot and mix well. Make sure to remove the onion and lemon slices from your chicken before you put it back in pot with sauce. Stir and heat for a few minutes put on serving plates, sprinkle with sesame seeds and chives serve it warm.

Chapter 6:
Pressure Cooker Vegetable Recipes 26-30

26. Stuffed Tomatoes

Total Time Needed: **15 minutes**

Ingredients:

- four fresh medium sized tomatoes
- one tablespoon of organic butter
- one small onion, finely chopped
- one teaspoon of pepper
- one teaspoon of salt

- one cup of low-fat cottage cheese
- one slice of whole wheat bread, crumbled
- one cup of mushrooms, finely chopped
- two tablespoons of celery, finely chopped
- one cup of water
- one tablespoon of parsley, fresh, chopped
- one teaspoon of cumin

Directions:

Cut the tomatoes stem to bottom, cutting the tip off each, then put aside. Using a spoon hollow out the tomatoes and put the pulp into a saucepan. Melt butter, add onion, and celery and stir-fry until the onion gets glossy. Add mushrooms. Cook until the liquid evaporates, stirring occasionally. Add all the other ingredients except for water. Divide into four portions and fill the tomatoes with it. Cover with the cut top of tomatoes. Pour the water into the pressure cooker, place the inset into the pressure cooker. Place the tomatoes on the insert. Close the pressure cooker and bring to full power over high heat. Immediately remove the pressure cooker from the heat and reduce the pressure placing the cooker in about two inches of water in sink for about two minutes. Open the pressure cooker and serve warm.

27. Stuffed Green Peppers

Total Time Needed: 15 minutes

Ingredients:

- four green peppers
- one cup of water

Vegetarian filling:

- two cups of cheddar cheese, grated
- one teaspoon of black pepper
- one teaspoon of sea salt
- four tablespoons of tomato, finely chopped, and peeled
- one quarter of a red onion, grated
- one cup of long grain rice, boiled

Or Tuna filling:

- one can of tuna, drained, in pieces
- two cups of cheddar cheese, grated
- one teaspoon of black pepper
- one teaspoon of sea salt
- one cup of mushrooms, finely chopped
- one quarter of a red onion, grated
- one cup of long grain rice, boiled

Directions:

Cut a hole around the tail of the peppers and remove the seed core from them gently. Rinse the core of peppers out to remove remaining seeds. Mix all of your filling ingredients in a bowl (vegetarian or tuna) except for one-cup of cheese. Divide your filling into four portions and stuff each pepper with the filling, knead filling well. Pour water into the pressure cooker and place the inset into it. Place your peppers onto the inset. Close the pressure cooker and bring to full power over high heat. Reduce heat to medium and cook for one minute. Remove the pressure cooker from the heat, reduce the pressure by placing pot into two inches of water in the sink for about two minutes. Open the pressure cooker and remove the peppers. Sprinkle the remaining cheese on top of the peppers. Bake the peppers in the oven for five minutes or until the cheese melts, serve warm.

28. Spicy Paneer

Total Time Needed: 10 minutes

Ingredients:

- one red onion, grated
- twelve ounces of green peas
- seven ounces of Paneer cheese, cubed
- a pinch of turmeric
- a few coriander leaves, chopped for garnish
- sea salt to taste
- four tablespoons of coconut oil
- one teaspoon of cumin
- one teaspoon of coriander powder
- one teaspoon of chili powder
- one inch of ginger, chopped
- two medium tomatoes, chopped

Directions:

In a saucepan lightly fry the Paneer cheese. In the pressure cooker, preheat the oil and slightly brown the onion. Add the ginger and one cup of water then add the tomatoes, spices, and fry until the fat separates. Add peas and fry for two minutes then pour in half a cup of water. Close the lid of pressure cooker and bring to full power over high heat. Reduce the heat to medium and cook for three minutes. Remove the pressure cooker and release the steam. Open and add the Paneer cheese, then cook for another two minutes. Serve sprinkled with chopped coriander leaves.

29. Curry

Total Time Needed: 10 minutes

Ingredients:

- one large red onion, grated
- seven ounces of peas, hulled
- two red potatoes, peeled, and cubed
- one large pinch of turmeric
- one teaspoon of ground cumin
- one teaspoon of ground coriander
- one teaspoon of chili powder
- one inch of ginger, chopped
- one large tomato, chopped
- three tablespoons of coconut oil
- sea salt to taste
- coriander leaves, as garnish

Directions:

Preheat your oil in the pressure cooker and then add onions, ginger, add tomato after five minutes add the peas, potatoes, spices, and salt. Stir-fry for three minutes. Add two cups of water. Close the pressure cooker bringing to full power over high heat. Reduce the heat to medium and cook for three minutes. Remove the pressure cooker from the heat and leave to cool slowly. Serve with coriander leaves as a garnish.

30. Egg, Corn Soup

Total Time Needed: 40 minutes

Ingredients:

- four fresh corn cobs
- one stalk of celery, chopped
- one red pepper, thinly sliced
- two tablespoons of cornstarch
- two eggs, soaked in boiling water for a moment
- salt and pepper to taste
- one teaspoon of Worcestershire sauce
- one teaspoon of peanut oil
- two chives, chopped for garnishing

Directions:

Mix your cornstarch in a little bit of water. In the pressure cooker boil 500 ml of water; add the corncobs, red pepper, celery, and salt and pepper. Close the pressure cooker and bring to full power over high heat. Reduce the heat to medium and cook for 15 minutes. Remove the pressure cooker from the heat and cool slowly. Open pressure cooker and strain the broth into a separate pot. Cut the kernels of corn from the cobs and add to the broth put on low heat. Add and mix cornstarch and water, Worcestershire sauce, peanut oil. Stir thoroughly. Cook for another 15 minutes on low heat. At the end add the eggs, and beat them with a fork.

Serve warm with chili sauce and soy sauce. Then sprinkle chopped chives on top of soup for garnish.

Bonus Pressure Cooker Desert Recipes!

Date & Apple Pudding

Total Time Needed: one hour

Ingredients:

- one cup of walnuts, chopped
- one cup of dates, chopped
- one large apple, peeled, and sliced
- one cup plus one teaspoon of sugar
- three cups of almond flour
- one teaspoon of allspice
- one teaspoon of cinnamon
- one teaspoon of nutmeg

- two eggs
- three cups of water
- two tablespoons of coconut oil
- one teaspoon of baking powder

Directions:

Mix the dates with apple, nuts and one cup of sugar (sugar can be replaced by sugar substitute such as Stevia). Mix flour, baking soda, salt, spice blend, cinnamon, nutmeg, then add to fruits and mix well. In a separate bowl, beat the eggs with oil, add to the other ingredients and mix well. Put the mixture into mold greased with butter, sprinkle with remaining sugar, and tightly cover with aluminum foil. Pour three cups of water into the pressure cooker, put in the inset and place the mold on top of it. Close the pressure cooker, but do not put the vent weight on. Cook over high heat until the valve begins to emit steam. Reduce the heat and be sure the steam is still escaping from the vent; cook for 15 minutes. After this apply weight valve and bring to full power boiling over high heat. Reduce heat to medium and cook for 40 minutes. Remove the pressure cooker from the heat and leave to cool slowly. Open the pressure cooker and remove the mold and gently remove the pudding from the mold using a knife. Put a plate on mold then turn upside down and shake gently to get the pudding out of mold. Serve warm or chilled.

Lemon Creme

Total Time Needed: 10 minutes

Ingredients:

- one egg
- one cup of milk
- one tablespoon of sugar or sugar replacement such as Stevia
- one teaspoon of lemon peel, grated
- one teaspoon of lemon juice
- tiny pinch of salt
- three cups of water
- whipped cream for garnish

Directions:

Bring the milk to boil and cool down. In a bowl whisk the eggs with the sugar, peel, and lemon juice as well as the salt. Mix well and slowly add the milk. Heat two heat resistant molds with butter and pour the cream into them. Cover tightly with aluminum foil. Pour water into the pressure cooker, put in the inset, and arrange the molds on top of it. Close the pressure cooker lid and bring to full power over high heat. Reduce heat to medium and cook for five minutes. Remove from heat and place in cold water about two inches for two minutes in sink. Remove the lid from pressure cooker and take out molds and remove the foil. Put aside to cool, then put into the fridge to chill, add spoonful of whipped cream just before serving, then enjoy!

Carrot Halva

Total Time Needed: five minutes

Ingredients:

- 15 ounces of carrots, grated
- seven ounces of condensed unsweetened milk
- four ounces of sugar or sugar substitute such as Stevia
- ten almonds, peeled
- one ounce of ghee
- one teaspoon of cardamom powder

Directions:

Put the carrot into the pressure cooker. Close the pressure cooker and bring to full power over high heat. Open immediately after the release of the accumulated steam. Add milk, ghee, and sugar. Fry until the carrots are slightly browned. Serve Sprinkled with chopped almonds and cardamom.

Chocolate Souffle

Total Time Needed: 20 minutes

Ingredients:

- one ounce of butter
- five eggs
- five fluid ounces of milk
- four ounces of chocolate
- five drops of vanilla essence
- one teaspoon of sugar powder
- two tablespoons of almond flour

Directions:

Grease your pudding mold with non-stick cooking spray. Break the chocolate and melt boiling milk. Cool down. In a saucepan melt the butter, add flour, and fry for a few minutes. Add the milk with chocolate and stir until it thickens. Let it cool down for a bit, add one egg yolk at a time. Add vanilla essence and sugar. At the end, mix gently with rigidly beaten egg whites. Transfer to mold and cover with greased baking paper. Pour six ounces of water into the pressure cooker and put in the inset and place the mold on top of it. Close the pressure cooker and bring to full power over high heat. Reduce the heat to medium and cook for 15 minutes. Remove the pressure cooker from the heat and leave to cool slowly. Open the pressure cooker and remove the paper, put and inverted plate on the mold, turn it upside down, gently shake. Garnish top with powdered sugar and enjoy!

Apple Walnut Bread Desert

Total Time Needed: 30 minutes

Ingredients:

- eight ounces of stale bread
- half a cup of water
- half a cup of sugar or sugar substitute such as Stevia
- two tablespoons of rum
- 500 grams of apples, peeled, cores removed, seeded
- powdered sugar for garnish
- two tablespoons of walnuts, crushed

Directions:

Grease the non-perforated inset with butter and arrange bread loafs on it; cover the bread with apple slices, walnuts, drizzle with sugar and cinnamon and tiny bits of butter, then place the next layer of bread, apples etc., until you run out of ingredients. Press well and then drizzle with water and rum. Cover with a piece of baking paper and then with a tiny plate. Put the inset into pressure cooker. Make sure to pour two cups of water at the bottom of the pressure cooker. Close the pressure cooker and come to full power over high heat. Reduce heat to medium and cook for 25 minutes. Remove the pressure cooker from heat and allow to cool slowly. Sprinkle top of apple, cake, bread with powdered sugar for garnish and enjoy!

Conclusion

I hope you will have as much fun trying this collection of recipes as I did in putting them together. Baking and preparing meals is a great way to spend some time with your loved ones such as your children. Teaching them how to prepare meals is a lesson that is not only fun but also very yummy! Helping you to prepare a meal will build up your child's self-confidence and yours when you both get the thumbs up for a tasty meal that you prepared together! I wish you great fun and enjoyment (especially for your taste buds) in preparing and enjoying these tasty pressure cooker recipes!

Thanks again for reading my book I would greatly appreciate it if you would be so kind as to leave a small review of my book—it would help me out a lot—I hope you will continue to read my collection of cookbooks!

I wish you the best of luck and enjoy your new Pressure Cooker recipes. Happy Cooking!

Eric Deen

Book 2
Dump Dinners: 30 Of The Most Delicious, Simple and Healthy Dump Dinner Recipes For You and Your Family!

Introduction

Ready to learn 30 Delicious, Healthy and Simple Dump dinner Recipes?

The dumped dinner recipes are a great source of nutrients for everyone as they are not having any sort of extra oil or over cooked ingredients which may destroy all the nutritional values of a dish. The process of making dumped recipes are very much different from the ones which we make usually in our daily routine. It involves slow cooking by dumping all the ingredients in a slow cooker until all the ingredients become ready to eat. One of the of the main reasons of saying the dumped recipes not only to be flavorful but nutritious as well is that it does not involve over cooking of all the ingredients as over cooking may result in losing all the nutritional values associated with each ingredient being used for making a particular dish.

Once you start having dumped recipes in your meal especially in dinner, you would not feel heavy and your health would also get improved by having these recipes in your dinner. This book is all about teaching you to make the best and unique dumped dinner recipes which you can make at your home without any problem. This is because, these recipes are very easy to be made and do not require any extra effort to be put in by you for making them all.

In this book you are going to have all the guidelines regarding making the delicious and easy dumped dinner recipes with so much simple ingredients. The recipes are being written in so simple language that you can comprehend the whole procedure easily without facing any sort of problem in understanding the procedure. As dumped recipes are mostly made in slow cookers so in this book you will also find the way by which you can use the slow cooker for making the dumped recipes easily.

Slow and dumped cooking helps you to save the essential nutrients of the ingredients which you use and thus the food which you eat has not been deprived of essential nutrients which are required for making you healthy and fit. This book has got 30 super delicious recipes for you which you can make easily by following the exact ingredients and directions that have been added. All the steps for making a particular dish has been elaborated so well that you can simply follow the recipe by following the step by step procedure.

You will feel no problem while acting upon the steps for making 30 delicious recipes as all the steps are aided with so much simple language that you can follow them easily.

The first half of the book is equipped with 15 delicious and easy to make dumped dinner starters which you can make to serve before serving the main course dumped meal.

In the second half of book, you will find the unique and delicious dumped dinner recipes which you can serve as a main course meal. All the recipes are very easy to be understood and there is no need of adding any extra step or ingredient as all the directions are well elaborated.

So, enjoy all the tasty dumped dinner recipe and after trying these recipes you will definitely want to try all of these again and again.

What are the dump dinners?

The plan for dump dinner includes all those recipes which are made in slow cooker by dumping all the ingredients together in the cooker for an hour or as per the requirement of a particular dish. The dump recipes are very easy to be made and you do not require to pit any extra effort to learn them as they are already too much easy to comprehend without any ambiguity.

The dump recipes include all types of meals like beef, chicken, dairy products, carbohydrates, spices and numerous vegetables etc. All of these ingredients can be combined together to make a super classic dump dish which is full of nutrition.

The main reason why these recipes are full of nutritional values lie in the fact that these recipes are not cooked on high flame as cooking the recipes on high flame may result in loss of all the nutritional values which a particular ingredient has. As, these recipes are cooked on low flame by dumping the ingredients for a long time, the nutritional value of all the used ingredients does not get lost in any case. So you get a dish which is delicious, easy to make and full of nutritional value.

Do not opt for those recipes which may not be beneficial for your health. So, you must give a try to the dump recipes which you can use as a starter or a main course dish in dinner. These dumped dinner dishes would be loved by you and you would like to have them again and again.

Chapter 1:
The dump dinner 15 Starter Recipes

Dump diner recipes are very east to be made and for making these easy and delicious recipes, all you have to do is to dump and cook. They are so much easy that in your hectic daily routine, you can easily make all of these recipes and save time as well. Here are some dump dinner recipes for making easy and delicious starters for your dinner.

1. Apple Betty Pie

Ingredients:

- One cup thin sliced apples
- 2 tablespoon all-purpose floor
- Pinch of lemon zest
- 1 teaspoon lemon juice
- 1 teaspoon cinnamon powder
- Half cup granulated sugar
- 2 cup bread crumbs (soft)
- 1 cup melted butter

Directions:

Take a bowl and put all ingredients in it except bread crumbs and butter. Mix all the ingredients well. In another bowl combine bread crumbs and butter and mix well. Take a cooker and make the first layer of mixture of bread crumbs and butter. Make the second layer of the mixture of rest of the ingredients. Repeat the process till three to four layers are formed. After that, cover the mixtures and cook for about 15 minutes till it becomes bubbly and brown.

2. Apple with butter

Ingredients:

- Quarter teaspoon cloves
- Sliced apples 1 cup
- Cinnamon half teaspoon
- Sugar 2 tablespoon
- Butter 4 tablespoon

Directions:

Take all the ingredients in a bowl except butter and mix them well. Take a slow cooker and add butter in it. Add rest of the ingredients and cover for about an hour till the apples become smooth. Serve hot.

3. Meat ball starter

Ingredients:

- Beef mince 1 cup
- Tomato ketchup 4 tablespoon
- Cinnamon half teaspoon
- Black pepper half teaspoon
- Salt as required
- Oil 2 tablespoon
- Lemon juice 2 tablespoon
- Hot sauce 2 tablespoon
- Bread crumbs 1 cup
- Butter 2 tablespoon

Directions:

Mix all the ingredients in a bowl and marinate for about an hour. Make meat balls of medium size. Take 2 eggs and beat them well. Dip balls in eggs followed by coating with bread crumbs. Dump in slow cooker along with butter for about four hours till the balls become soft and juicy.

4. Santa Chicken

Ingredients:

- Boneless chicken half kg cubed
- Black beans boiled half cup
- Sweet corn half cup
- Red chilli sauce 3 tablespoon
- Olive oil 2 tablespoon
- Salt as required

Directions:

Heat the olive oil in slow cooker. Take a bowl and pit all ingredients in it and mix them well. Marinate for about half an hour. Add the mixture in to the pre heated olive oil, damp in cooker for about an hour. Serve hot.

5. Shrimp cheese chowder

Ingredients:

- Half cup cheddar cheese
- Half cup mozzarella cheese
- Shrimps boiled 1 cup
- Cinnamon 1 teaspoon
- Soy sauce 2 tablespoon
- Vinegar 2 tablespoon
- Red pepper flakes 1 teaspoon

Directions:

Take shrimps, add all the ingredients in them except cheese. Mix them well in a bowl and leave for about 2 hours. Take a dump cooker, add shrimps in it. Put a layer of cheddar cheese on it followed by placing a layer of mozzarella cheese. Cover the cooker and cook for about 2 hours till the shrimps become tender and cheese gets brown. Serve hot and enjoy.

6. Eggplant fiesta

Ingredients:

- 1 cup egg plant (cubed)
- Half cup onion chopped
- Half cup celery
- 3 tablespoon olive oil
- Vinegar 4 tablespoon
- Salt as required
- Red chili sauce 2 tablespoon
- Soy sauce half tablespoon

Directions:

Using a bowl, take all the ingredients except olive oil and mix them well so that the mixture becomes consistent. Marinate for about 2 hours so that the sauces get enriched inside. Take a slow cooker and add olive oil till hot. Add rest of the ingredients. Cover the pot for dumping all the ingredients and cook for an hour till the eggplant becomes soft.

7. Chicken boneless salsa

Ingredients:

- One cup of shredded coconut
- One cup chicken boneless (cubed)
- Mustard sauce 2 tablespoon
- Salt as required
- Black pepper 2 teaspoon
- Corn flour 2 tablespoon
- Vinegar 2 tablespoon
- Half a teaspoon of baking powder

Directions:

Take a bowl and add chicken, mustard sauce, black pepper, shredded coconut, vinegar and rest of the spices and mix all the ingredients well. Take a slow cooker, add the mixture in it along with the olive oil. Add corn flour to make it thicker. Cook for about an hour till the gravy becomes thicker and chicken becomes soft.

8. Potato casserole

Ingredients:

- Potatoes boiled and mashed 4 medium sized
- 2 beaten eggs
- Milk half cup
- Cheddar cheese 1 cup
- Mozzarella cheese half cup
- Black pepper half a teaspoon
- Salt as required
- Vinegar 2 teaspoon
- Hot sauce 2 tablespoon

Directions:

Take a slow cooker and add milk and beaten eggs. Stir for few minutes and then add potatoes and rest of the ingredients except cheddar and mozzarella cheese. Mix them well and add cheese at the end from top. Cover the cooker and dump the ingredients for about an hour. Serve hot.

9. Dumped cola chicken flurry

Ingredients:

- Chicken boneless half a kg (cubed)
- Onion powder 2 tablespoon
- Cream of mushroom soup mix 1 pack
- Water 2 tablespoon

Directions:

Take cubed chicken and pit random cuts on the surface for making it to marinate from deep inside. Take onion powder and sprinkle it on the chicken and by taking help of hands, try to put the onion powder inside the cuts a well. Add cream of mushroom soup mix to chicken along with some water so that it takes the form of a gravy. Dump it in the cola can and cook on low heat for about 4 hours. Serve hot with green chilli sauce.

10. Stir fried dumped eggs

Ingredients:

- Five eggs
- Two teaspoons of olive oil
- Quarter a cup of chopped green capsicum
- Two cups of boiled spinach
- Two teaspoon of onion powder
- 2 teaspoon of mustard powder
- Two teaspoons of minced garlic
- One teaspoon of black pepper

Directions:

Heat olive oil in the slow cooker. Take a mixing bowl and mix all the ingredients very well. Beat eggs and pour the mixed ingredients in it. Take this mixture in the pre heated oil in slow cooker and dump for about half an hour till the eggs becomes soft. Enjoy.

11. Dumped beef with potatoes

Ingredients:

- Half a cup boneless beef
- Two potatoes medium sized
- Half a teaspoon of black pepper
- Salt as required
- Two onion medium sized
- Vinegar two tablespoon

Directions:

Take the potatoes and onion and place them at the bottom of slow cooker. Take a bowl and add all the ingredients in it along with beef and marinate for about 20 minutes. Add the marinated beef over already placed onions and potatoes in the slow cooker. Cover the cooker and dump for about two hours till the beef becomes soft and tender. Serve hot with chilli garlic sauce.

12. Dumped sausage light casserole

Ingredients:

- Half a cup of chopped sausages
- 2 medium sized boiled potatoes
- Two medium sized tomatoes sliced
- half a cup green onion
- Four eggs
- Salt as required
- Black pepper as required
- Onion powder two tablespoon
- Cheddar cheese half a cup

Directions:

Pre heat the slow cooker. On the other side take a bowl and add eggs in it. Add all the ingredients in eggs except cheese and sausages. Beat them well till fluffy. Now add olive oil to the slow cooker, add diced sausages and dump for about half an hour. Uncover the cooker and add beaten eggs followed by the addition of cheddar cheese. Cover again the cooker for about an hour till the eggs become completely cooked and cheese become bubbly and brown.

13. Dumped spinach omelet

Ingredients:

- Half a cup of boiled spinach
- Dry coriander two teaspoon
- One teaspoon of olive oil
- Six eggs
- 2 medium tomatoes sliced
- Cheddar cheese half a cup
- Vinegar 4 tablespoon
- Salt as required
- Red chili sauce 2 tablespoon
- Soy sauce half tablespoon

Directions:

Take all the ingredients in a bowl except cheese and mix them well. Beat the eggs in a separate bowl and add them to the mixture of ingredients. Pre heat the slow cooker, add olive oil and add the beaten eggs in it while stirring continuously. Add cheese at the end and mix well again. Cover the cooker and dump for about an hour till all the ingredients become soft and tender.

14. Spinach chicken with ginger

Ingredients:

- Ginger paste 2 tablespoon
- Potato 2 boiled
- Spring onion 1 cup chopped
- Green onion 2 chopped
- Chicken boneless half cup boiled
- Cheese 1 cup
- Capsicum 1 chopped
- Carrots 2 chopped
- Oil 2 tablespoon
- Pepper as required

Directions:

Preheat the slow cooker and add oil and heat for about five minutes. Now add all the vegetables and mix them well. Add boneless chicken along with all the spices and mix all ingredients well. Add cheese at end and dump the cooker for about one and a half hour till all the ingredients become completely cooked. Serve hot.

15. Dumped macaroni with mushrooms

Ingredients:

- Macaroni 1 packet (boiled)
- Mushrooms half a cup (chopped)
- Olive oil 2 teaspoon
- Salt as required
- Pepper as required
- Red chilli sauce two tablespoon
- Soy sauce 2 tablespoon
- Cheese 1 cup
- Milk half cup
- Cream half cup

Directions:

Take a slow cooker and turn the heat on and pre heat the cooker for about 15 minutes. Take a bowl and combine all the ingredients except oil and leave them for about 10 minutes. Add oil to the cooker followed by addition of the rest of the ingredients and dump for about an hour till the cheese becomes brown and bubbly. Uncover the cooker and serve the yummy dish with green or red chilli sauce and mustard sauce.

Chapter 2:
The dumped dinner 20 main course recipes

This chapter has 20 delicious and mouth-watering dumped dinner main course recipes which should be given a must try. These recipes are not only easy to be made but they are enriched in so many nutrients that are beneficial for your health as well. So, enjoy the unique collection of dumped dinner delicious main course recipes.

1. Dumped chicken onion

Ingredients:

- Olive oil 2 table spoon
- Onion 2
- Salt and black pepper
- Potatoes 1
- Butter half a cup
- Tomato paste half a cup
- Ginger and garlic 2 tablespoon each
- Fresh thyme 1 table spoon
- Worcestershire sauce 2 teaspoon
- Chicken boneless half a cup boiled and shredded
- Toasted almonds half a cup

Directions:

Add all the ingredients in a bowl except oil. Mix them well until all the sauces and spices becomes consistent. Pre heat the cooker for about half an hour and add oil in it till it becomes hot. Add the mixture from bowl in to the pre heated oil and cover the cooker. Dump the cooker for about an hour till it gets ready. Serve hot with garlic sauce and mayonnaise.

2. Baked eggs with bacons

Ingredients:

- Six slices bacons
- Teaspoon bacon drippings two
- Four eggs
- One diced tomato
- Half a cup of chopped onions
- Four medium sized chopped mushrooms
- Half a tea spoon of black pepper
- Salt as required
- Two teaspoon of mustard sauce

Directions:

Pre heat the slow cooker. Take a bowl and mix tomatoes, onion, and mushrooms and all spices. You may fill the inside circle of the bacon with the above mentioned mixture. Break the eggs and cover up the mushroom with the egg. Add them to the pre heated slow cooker and dump for about an hour till it gets ready to serve. Garnish with additional mustard sauce if you want. Serve hot.

3. Dumped spicy ribs

Ingredients:

- One onion chopped
- Two teaspoons of olive or sunflower oil
- Salt as required
- Coriander leaves 2 tablespoon
- Beef short ribs: 3 Ibs
- One chopped carrot
- Three cloves garlic chopped
- A cup of beef stock
- 1 cup water
- Figs 10 chopped
- 2 tablespoon lemon juice

Directions:

Heat the olive oil in pre heated slow cooker.
Mediante ribs with salt, lemon juice, garlic and red sauce then add garlic, onion and carrot and leave for about half an hour to get it marinated. Pour water and dump in slow cooker for four hours till the ribs become soft. Serve hot with green chili sauce.

4. Dumped chicken with creamy sauce

Ingredients:

- Three chicken breasts
- One red pepper chopped
- Two medium sized onions chopped
- Half a cup of chopped green onion
- Salt and pepper as required
- One teaspoon of paprika
- Half a cup of chopped coriander and mint leaves
- Three tablespoons of olive oil
- 5 tablespoons butter
- 5 large garlic cloves
- A cup of chicken broth
- 5 oz cream cheese
- A cup of heavy cream
- Two teaspoon Weber Canadian Chicken Seasoning

Directions:

Over medium heat, shallow fry the onions and garlic in a pan in butter until soft. Remove from skillet and set aside. Pre heat the slow cooker and add butter and melt over low heat. Add cream cheese and stir until melted and mixed with the wine and butter. Add cream and rest of the ingredients and stir until mixed. Add chicken to slow cooker in a single layer. Add the onion mixture over the chicken in even proportions. Add the cream sauce mixture over chicken and onions. Dump for about an hour till chicken becomes soft and tender. Serve hot.

5. Dumped chicken salsa

Ingredients:

- 2-3 tablespoons of butter
- A cup of white onion finely chopped
- 4 garlic cloves chopped
- 6 boneless chicken breast halves
- Two tomatoes chopped
- Two chopped green chilies
- 6 oz. full fat cream cheese
- A cup of whipped cream
- A cup of chicken broth
- 1 teaspoon dried cumin
- 2 teaspoon garlic powder to taste
- 1 teaspoon salt or as required
- Cheddar cheese for garnish
- Corn flour 2 tablespoon

Directions:

Wash and pat dry chicken breasts and cut in to cubes. In a slow cooker over medium heat, melt butter and stir fry the onions and garlic until software. Add chicken and cook all sides of slices until juices run clear. Decrease heat to medium low, and add tomatoes and chilies. Dump for two hours and allow chicken to simmer. Add cream cheese and cream after uncovering after two hours and stir until cheese is melted, and chicken and vegetables are coated. Add broth to thin if sauce is too thick. Dump for another half an hour and serve hot.

6. Dumped dinner meatballs

Ingredients:

- Three medium sized white onion chopped
- 4 tablespoon of butter
- 1 cup shredded cheddar cheese
- 2 beaten eggs
- Salt as required
- Freshly ground black pepper as required
- 2 teaspoons of herb seasonings
- Half a cup of cream cheese
- Half a cup of ground beef

Directions:

Preheat slow cooker for about 20 minutes. Add onions in butter in a separate pan until soft then remove from heat, and cool for 10 minutes. During this process in a mixing bowl, combine cheddar cheese and eggs. Whisk until smooth. Add the spices, salt, and pepper and mix well. Add onions and cream cheese and mix well. Add beef and mix until all ingredients get combined. Divide meat mixture into 1 ounce part. You should end up with about 25- 27 equal sized parts. Make balls of each part by your hands. Place the meatballs in the slow cooker and dump for about 90 minutes till the balls becomes juicy and soft. Serbe hot with mustard and chilli garlic sauce.

7. Strawberry dumped pancakes

Ingredients:

- Two Bananas diced
- 2 tablespoons of protein powder
- Four egg whites
- Two tablespoon of almond milk
- A cup of frozen or fresh strawberries
- Two tablespoon Cinnamon
- 4 tablespoons of Greek yogurt
- 1 teaspoon of honey

Directions:

Mash the bananas. Add the protein powder and all the ingredients except the strawberries in a bowl and stir really well. Now add the raspberries and stir. Spray the pre heated slow cooker with olive oil spray and pour the mix in it. Dump on medium heat for 10 minutes until the edges are brown and flip it followed by dumping again for 10 minutes. Cook until the middle is well cooked. Serve with cheese cream.

8. Savory dumped almond muffins

Ingredients:

- 1 cups of Almond Flour
- Half teaspoon of baking soda
- Salt a pinch
- 1 teaspoon of dried thyme
- 4 eggs beaten
- Half a cup of melted butter
- A cup of shredded cheddar cheese

Directions:

Preheat slow cooker for about 20 minutes. Take all the dry ingredients and mix them well. Add eggs and butter together and combine all the ingredients together. Add rest of the ingredients and stir until it gets consistent. Add mixture to the tray and place the tray in slow cooker and dump for about two and a half hours till the muffins become soft and tender.

9. Dumped eggs with sausages

Ingredients:

- 1 tablespoon butter
- Half a cup of chopped chicken sausages
- Three carrots peeled and striped
- A cup of chopped cauliflower
- A cup of finely chopped celery
- Two medium onions chopped into small pieces
- Six large eggs
- A cup of shredded cheddar cheese

Directions:

Slice the sausages. Over medium heat, melt the butter in a separate pan while place the slow cooker for pre heating on the other side. Add the vegetables and bacon in the pan. Stir all the ingredients and sauté the bacon and vegetables in the butter until the bacon starts to crisp on the edges and the vegetables begin to caramelize. Spread the mixture in the slow cooker. Break one egg into each well. Continue cooking until the eggs are almost done. Cover the slow cooker and let the eggs steam until cooked through. Sprinkle cheese over and dump for about an hour till all the ingredients become cooked well. Serve hot.

10. Dumped dinner cheese cookies

Ingredients:

- Two cups of all-purpose flour
- Half a cup of cheddar cheese
- Half a cup of mozzarella cheese
- Four tablespoons of butter
- Half a cup of cream cheese
- 4 Eggs beaten
- Four teaspoon of fresh black pepper
- Two teaspoon of baking soda
- Salt a pinch

Directions:

Preheat the slow cooker for about an hour. Mix the all-purpose flour and both kinds of cheese in a processor till the mixture becomes consistent. Melt down the crème cheese and butter on low flame till both becomes smooth. Add baking soda and salt in beaten eggs. Mix all the above mentioned mixtures together one by one till smooth. Put the cookie sheet in the pre heated slow cooker and cover it for making it dumped for about an hour. Serve till the cookies gets cool at room temperature.

11. Simple dumped dinner eggs

Ingredients:

- Four tablespoons of butter
- Three large eggs
- 1 cup grated cheddar cheese
- 1 cup grated mozzarella or parmesan cheese
- Half a cup of heavy cream
- Six slices cooked bacon
- Salt as required
- Black pepper as required

Directions:

Preheat the slow cooker for about an hour. Break the eggs in to a pan which is going to be placed in slow cooker later. Cover each egg with mozzarella and cheddar cheese and cream and add salt and pepper to taste in it. Place the pan in the slow cooker and dump for about an hour until the cheese is melted and the egg whites are mostly done. Crumble two slices of cooked bacon over each egg and serve at once.

12. Dumped chicken quiche

Ingredients:

- Two cups of cheddar cheese
- Four tablespoons butter
- 2 medium white onion chopped
- Six large eggs preferably organic
- A cup of heavy cream
- Salt as required
- 1 teaspoon of black or white pepper
- 2 teaspoon of dried thyme
- A cup of chicken boiled and shredded

Directions:

Preheat the slow cooker an hour before using it. In a separate pan, add butter and melt over medium heat. Add the vegetables and stir fry until onions are soft. Remove from heat and cool.

Take a pan and apply butter on it. Put shredded cheese in bottom of the buttered pan. Add cooled vegetable mixture to the in an even layer over cheese. Crack the eggs and pour into a large mixing bowl. Add the cream and spices, and whisk together. Pour half the mixture over each pan of cheese and vegetables then use a fork to gently and evenly distribute cheese and vegetables into egg and cream mixture. Slide pan into the slow cooker and dump for about half an hour or until set and puffy and slightly golden in the center. You can also use a knife to insert into middle of one of the quiches, and if it comes out clean, they are done. Serve immediately, or cool and refrigerate or freeze.

13. Dumped raspberry muffins

Ingredients:

- Three cups of Almond Flour
- Two cups of heavy cream
- Six eggs
- A cup of melted butter
- A pack of artificial sweetener
- Half teaspoon of baking soda
- A teaspoon of lemon extract
- One teaspoon dried lemon zest
- Salt as required
- Fresh or frozen raspberries one cup

Directions:

Preheat the slow cooker for two hours. Take a separate bowl and Mix almond flour and cream in it. Add eggs one at a time, and stir until mixed. Add butter, sweetener, baking soda, flavoring and spices and mix. Add raspberries and stir until evenly distributed. Spoon mixture into pan, filling each cupcake paper about half full. Place the pan in the slow cooker and dump for about an hour till the muffins become soft and tender.

14. Dumped corn bread

Ingredients:

- Half cup of butter milk
- Baking soda 2 teaspoon
- Corn meal 1 cup
- Salt as required
- Half a cup of all-purpose flour
- One teaspoon of honey

Directions:

Preheat the slow cooker and at the same time take a bowl and mix all ingredients in it. Transfer the ingredients to a pan and put the pan in slow cooker. Dump for about half an hour till the bread becomes brown.

15. Dumped Cheese bread

Ingredients:

- A cup of almond flour
- Half a teaspoon of baking powder
- Salt a pinch
- A cup of cream cheese
- Half a cup of shredded cheddar cheese
- Half a cup of shredded mozzarella cheese
- Four tablespoons butter
- 2 eggs large beaten
- Half a cup of water (preferably Luke warm)

Directions:

Take a bowl and mix all the dry ingredients together one by one. In a separate glass bowl, soften the cream cheese and butter till smooth. Let the mixture gets cooled. Now combine all the ingredients together and add water. Mix well. Use a spoon for placing the mixture and place the scoops in to the glazed pan. Dump the mixture for an hour until the bread becomes soft and brown. Serve.

Conclusion

I am completely hoping that you will definitely enjoy all the dumped dinner recipes which I have added in this book. I am glad to say here that all the recipes which have been included in this book are totally healthy and full of nutritional values. No junk or artificial food items are used in any of the recipes which I have added in this book. I have added 30 delicious dumping recipes to be made at dinner and you will enjoy having every bite of them for sure.

In the first chapter I have added the basic information about dumped recipes for your information if you do not know already that what the dumped recipes are. After that I have thrown light on the importance of these recipes and have told you the way by which you can make these recipes easily by using slow cookers.

Throwing light on the importance is followed by sharing with you 15 dumped dinner starter recipes which you can make very easily. The next chapter includes the 15 main course recipes which I hope would must become the part of your every dinner.

Finally, if you enjoyed this book, then I'd like to ask you for a **big favor**, would you be kind enough to leave a review for this book on Amazon? It'd be greatly appreciated! I wish you the best of luck and enjoy your new healthy Dump Dinner recipes!

Eric Deen

Book 3
The Clean Eating Diet: Over 30 Delicious and Healthy Clean Eating Recipes To Lose Weight, and Increase Energy Forever!

Introduction

For those living really unhealthy and inactive lifestyles, hearing about the concept of clean eating is like being given a death sentence. They treat this as a scare tactic to get them to move their bodies, start exercising and decreasing their total daily food intake. But in reality, cleaning eating should be that right kind of motivation for them to embark on a quest of finding and rediscovering their best selves.

The Clean Eating Cookbook is the perfect ally that you should have to make sure that you will be able to properly take on the challenge of giving your pantry, grocery list, your cooking and your food choices complete makeovers. How? Well, the book offers you tons of helpful bits of information, which can be very beneficial in ensuring that you will not only lose the weight that you have been trying to shed for many years, at the same time, you and your family will feel more energetic and will soon achieve the best state of health. The book offers:

- Over 30 delicious and really healthy recipes that could jumpstart your weight loss project. From appetizers all the way to your favorite desserts, this book has got your back covered.

- Top tips, including best clean eating practices that you and your family should know and live by. This includes how to start following a clean and healthy lifestyle and the ways to deal and possibly avoid the road blocks that you may or may not encounter.

- Detailed awareness of what clean eating is all about, the different principles that you should learn and practice by heart especially if you are seriously considering turning a new and a healthier "leaf" this year.

- The right kind of encouragement to start buying, cooking and of course, eating healthier and cleaner types of food.

The book aims to help those who needs just the right push to go for their dreams becoming healthier, more energetic and most of all, achieving their optimum health.

Chapter 1: What is Clean Eating

Sometimes, all you need to do is to backtrack your life and think about your eating habits back when your life was a lot simpler. People who have jumped from one weight loss regimen to another are there to attest that for these diets to work, you need to start cleaning up your eating habits. Because amidst the different exercise routines and the diet fads that have gained popularity over the years, once thing is for sure, they all start and end with food!

What is Clean Eating?

The concept of clean eating has been practiced ever since the first man learned how to make use of the natural vegetation and wild animal resources in their areas. It is simply eating organic, lean and naturally obtained fruits, vegetables and meat using the simplest and the healthiest preparations.

Contrary to what most people believe, this practice is not a diet. But rather, clean eating is a lifestyle. This is not something that you can follow just to lose weight and forego once you have achieved your weight loss goals. Eating clean is a practice that you and your family should ultimately live by for the rest of your lives.

To better understand what this healthy lifestyle is all about, you definitely need to find out more about its principles.

The Principles of Clean Eating

Clean eating involves specific principles that does not just cover choosing the healthiest of fruits, vegetables and cuts of meat. It also requires the ability to completely avoid the consumption of certain types of food in order for this new found love for health to work.

- **Cook your own food** – meals prepared at home are known and proven to be several times healthier than your favorite fast food meals. No matter how much these restaurants claim that they use nothing but the best products, you can never be too sure that they do not use processed food products. Clean eating will help you learn how to prepare fast, simple and healthy meals.

- **Consume Whole Foods** – these are food items that have not been altered or laced with fertilizers and other growth inducing chemicals. Think about the concept of "Farm to Table Meals" and you will understand that this is about choosing completely organic and farm raised products.

- **No to Processed Foods** – canned, packed and labeled foods are considered to be processed types of food. The thing about such types of foods is that they may contain ingredients, such as preservatives that could be chemically laced and are harmful to your body. But if there are processed foods that you can eat, those would be whole grain pastas, vegan meat substitutes, organic grains and flours and cheeses. Every time you read the labels, keep in mind that if you cannot pronounce it, do not buy it!

- **Eat Five or Six Meals Everyday** – now this should be done in moderation, to make sure that your body will have enough fuel to burn. These meals should be small and should ultimately be healthy.

- **Having the Right Combination of Carbs and Protein** – this will encourage you to go for more balanced meals every single day. Whether you are snacking or having lunch, your plate should have the right proportions of carbs and protein. This will not only make your healthier, you will also be able to quell all your bouts of hunger and unrealistic cravings.

- **Say No to Refined Sugar** – these are chemically produced, which means that they are harmful and can cause your blood sugar level to dangerously increase.

Through these principles, you will be able to create a more solid and healthy eating habit.

Chapter 2:
Benefits of Clean Eating

Now that you know what clean eating is all about, it is time for you to become fully aware of the benefits that you and your family can get out of choosing the types of food you eat and the way you consume food, in general. So what can clean eating do to your body and your overall health?

- **Helps regulates your digestive system's processes** – have you noticed that after eating that large serving of cheese burger and a handful of fries, your stomach feels so full and totally acidic? Well, if you observe carefully, you will even hear your digestive enzymes struggle to work their way through all the oily processed foods that you have consumed. Clean eating will help put a stop to acid refluxes, indigestion and poor bowel movement.

You will have all the fiber that you need to improve your digestion in so many ways.

- **Helps keep you satisfied for longer periods of time** – junk food makes you crave more food, which in turn makes you gain those unwanted pounds. Eating cleaner and healthier food will make sure that you will feel full and satisfied longer since you will be completely nourished.

- **Helps you stay active and energized** – foods that are high in cholesterol can slow you down, not to mention that they can cause serious health problems. But with whole foods, you will be able to not only decrease your cholesterol levels, you will also have enough energy to go through your day from start to finish.

- **Helps keep your body nourished and healthy** – at the end of the day, your main goal is to be healthy, so following a clean eating lifestyle will help you achieve that, plus more. The body will have the energy and the capacity to breakdown your food, enough to extract the right amounts of nutrients and micronutrients to satiate your body's needs to achieve your optimum health. These foods will help lower your cholesterol levels, regulate your sugar intake and strengthen your immune system.

- **Helps you become adventurous and experimental in cooking** – this lifestyle does not mean that you have to eat bland and dull looking meals every single time. Clean eating, with all the amazingly healthy ingredients that you can choose from, should and will encourage you to try new recipes to bring life to your dishes. Clean eating should get you excited to prepare your own meals!

- **Clean eating is for the benefit of everyone**– gone are the days when you think that healthy or clean eating is just for vegans, vegetarians, diabetes, heart patients or those who are on a really strict diet. Clean eating is for those who would like to take great care of themselves better.

Chapter 3:
Clean Eating Lifestyle Tips to Follow When Preparing Your Food

Clean eating can sometimes be discouraging even for those who already know their way around the kitchen. For those who are just starting out, these tips can surely supersize your excitement to prepare your very own healthier versions of your favorite recipes, more so, to try new ones.

- **Spice Up Your Meals** – if you are a bit scared to try new spices and seasoning blends, why don't you go for herbs and other ingredients that could elevate and take your healthy meals to whole new levels? Try experimenting and incorporating these healthy herbs and spices in your next recipes:

- o   Cloves

- o   Cinnamon

- o   Nutmeg

- o   Cumin

- o   Turmeric

- o   Sage

- o   Mint

- o   Rosemary

- o   Basil

- o   Marjoram

- o   Chili

- o   Thyme

- **Plan your meals** – there are several ways to diversify your meals on a daily basis. Make the internet your best friend, or this book to look for amazingly delicious but unbelievably healthy dishes that you can easily make for your family. You can create a chart and plan what you will be cooking and eating for a week or in the next few days.

- **Experiment in the kitchen** – do not be afraid to get out of your comfort zone and experiment on different healthy recipes that you have found. You can try small portions first and see if you and the rest of the family will like what you have prepared.

- **Cook your meals ahead** – you really do not have to be a slave in the kitchen everyday, because there are healthy or nutritious meals that you can make ahead of time, store in the fridge and reheat. You can even label the containers with the dates or day that they should be consumed to keep their freshness and maintain their flavors.

- **Make a list** – do not get too overly excited to shop for fruits, veggies, meats and dairy products. Keep a record of what ingredients you have and take note of their expiration dates; this list will serve are your reference for the next time that you will go grocery shopping.

With all these in mind, it is definitely time to start cooking!

Chapter 4:
30 Amazing Recipes to Improve Your Health

Starting from your appetizers, you will now have the chance to really try following a healthier and cleaner lifestyle.

Healthy Appetizers You Should Try Making

Set the right tone for healthy eating by making these easy appetizer recipes:

Mozzarella, Basil and Tomato Skewers

Ingredients:

- 16 pieces of fresh buffalo mozzarella balls

- 16 pieces of cherry tomatoes

- 16 pieces of fresh basil leaves

- Olive oil

- Sea salt and freshly cracked black pepper

- Small skewers

Instructions

- Take a small skewer and thread a piece of mozzarella ball, a piece of basil leaf and a cherry tomato. Do this process until you have made 16 skewers and drizzle with olive oil. Season with salt and pepper.

Amp up the flavors by lightly grilling them.

Balsamic Tomato Bruschetta

Ingredients:

- 8 plum or Roma tomatoes de-seeded and diced
- 1/3 cup of basil chopped
- ¼ of parmesan cheese shredded
- 2 large garlic cloves minced
- 1 Tablespoons of high quality balsamic vinegar
- 1 teaspoon of olive oil
- ¼ teaspoon of sea or kosher salt
- ¼ teaspoon of black pepper
- 1 loaf of French bread sliced and toasted.

Instructions

- In a large bowl combine tomatoes, cheese, basil and garlic together. Add in the balsamic vinegar, olive oil, salt and pepper. Cover and let the mixture marinate in the fridge for at least 30 minutes to let the flavors marry together.

- Once ready to serve, toast the slices of French bread drizzled in olive oil. Spoon the marinated tomato mixture and serve.

Lemon and Thyme Ricotta Dip

Ingredients:

- 1 15 ounce container of fresh, part skim ricotta cheese
- 2 tablespoons of fresh thyme chopped
- 2 tablespoons of shallot, minced or chopped finely
- 1 teaspoon of fresh chives, chopped
- 2 teaspoons of lemon zest
- ¼ cup of freshly squeezed lemon juice
- ½ teaspoon of sea salt
- 1 teaspoon of black or white pepper
- 2 teaspoons of extra virgin olive oil

Instructions

- Using a blender, food processor or regular mixer, whip together the ricotta, thyme, chives, shallots, lemon zest and juice, salt and pepper until light and smooth.

- Place in a bowl and drizzle with 2 teaspoons of olive oil. Serve with fresh vegetables, wheat thins, naan or tortilla chips.

Easy Homemade Kale Chips

Ingredients:

- 1 large bunch of fresh kale
- 1 Tablespoon of olive oil
- 1 tablespoon of sherry vinegar
- 1/8 teaspoons of kosher or sea salt

Instructions

- Preheat your oven to 150 degrees Centigrade.

- Trim and prep your kale by taking the ribs out of each leaf. Dry the kale and drizzle with olive oil. Toss the leaves by hand to ensure that each is coated with oil. Sprinkle with vinegar and toss well.

- Line a baking sheet with a silicone baking sheet or parchment paper and evenly spread the leaves.

- Bake for about 35 minutes or until the chips are crispy.

- Season with salt and serve as is or with some homemade tartar sauce.

Goat Cheese Stuffed Tomatoes

Ingredients

- 24 pieces of cherry tomatoes
- 3 ounces of fresh goat cheese
- 1 tablespoon of low fat milk
- 2 tablespoons of chopped green or black olives
- 2 teaspoons of chopped oregano (fresh)
- 1/8 teaspoons of pepper

Instructions

- Slice the tops of each cherry tomato and scoop out the seeds (if any). Set aside and start preparing the filling.

- Mix the goat cheese, olives, milk, pepper and oregano together to form a paste.

Fill each tomato's cavity and drizzle with olive oil, more oregano and pepper. You can chill these before serving.

Healthy Black Bean Salsa

Ingredients

- 3 cans or about 3 and ½ cups of black beans. You can buy dried ones and cook them until tender
- 1 cup of Mexican corn or 1 can of corn
- 4 large fresh Roma tomatoes, diced
- 1 large green chili pepper (Jalapeno)
- ½ cup of green onions, chopped
- 1 bunch of cilantro leaves
- Salt and pepper to taste

Instructions

- Mix together all the ingredients, except for the cilantro leaves. If you want the cilantro taste to come together with the rest of the mixture, you may chop half of the bunch and toss it in. Season with salt and pepper.

- Place the mixture in a bowl, top with the remaining cilantro leaves and serve with tortilla, corn chips or crackers.

Crispy Polenta Wedges with Tomato Tapenade

Ingredients

- 1 tube of pre-made polenta (you can make your own by cooking polenta on a stove, according to package direction and spread onto a lined baking sheet and chill to solidify.)
- Cooking spray or canola oil
- 2/3 cup of sun dried tomatoes (canned or jarred)
- 4 teaspoons of olive oil
- 1 tablespoon of chopped flat-leaf parsley
- 2 teaspoons of capers, rinsed to remove the excess salt
- 1 garlic clove minced
- 1/8 teaspoons of pepper

Instructions

- Preheat your oven to 350 degrees and line a baking sheet with parchment paper and spray some non-stick cooking spray over the paper. You can also oil the sheet with canola oil.

- Slice the polenta into wedges or triangles and place them, evenly spaced, onto the baking pan. Bake the polenta wedges for about 15 minutes or until the edges are crispy and let them cool.

- In a food processor, blend the tomatoes parsley, garlic, olive oil, capers and pepper into a thick but not so smooth paste.

- Top each polenta wedge with the tomato tapenade, sprinkle parsley and serve.

Quick and Easy Hummus

Ingredients

- 1 can or about 15 ounces of cooked garbanzo beans or chick peas
- 2 ounces of fresh Jalapeno peppers, sliced into rounds
- ½ teaspoon of cumin (powder)
- 2 Tablespoons of lemon juice
- 3 large cloves of garlic, chopped

Instructions

- Using a food processor, combine all ingredients together to form a paste. If the mixture is too thick, add a little bit of the chickpea water. Keep adding until you have reached the desired consistency.

- Place the hummus in a bowl and serve with sliced flat bread, pita chips or paratha.

Thai-Style Chicken Balls

Ingredients

- 2 lbs of minced chicken
- 1 cup bread crumbs
- 4 green onions, chopped
- 1 tablespoons of coriander powder
- 1 cup of fresh cilantro, chopped
- ¼ cup of Thai sweet chili sauce
- 2 tablespoons of freshly squeezed lemon juice
- Canola oil for frying

Instructions

- In a bowl, mix together chicken, bread crumbs, chopped green onions, coriander powder, cilantro, chili sauce and lemon juice together. Form balls out of the mixture and set aside. Chill the prepared chicken balls to make sure that it is firm enough for frying.

- Meanwhile, heat oil in a deep pot or fryer. Once the chicken balls are firm enough, fry each ball in hot oil.

Steak and Blue Cheese Wrapped Bell Peppers

Ingredients

- 16 thinly sliced steak, grilled
- 1 cup of blue cheese or goat's cheese
- 4 large red and yellow bell peppers cut into strips.

Instructions

- Spread a generous amount of cheese onto each steak.

Place about 3 or 4 pepper strips on top of the cheese and roll each piece of steak to form a log. Secure each with a toothpick.

Entrees or Main Courses

Breakfast, lunch or dinner, the main course will always be the meal that will convince you and your family that healthy and clean eating is definitely the way to go.

Quick Tomato-Mozzarella Pizza

Ingredients

- 1 frozen whole wheat pizza dough (you can also use large tortillas or flat breads)
- 2 tablespoons of yellow cornmeal or course corn flour
- 5 large plum tomatoes, sliced thinly
- 1 large clove of garlic, minced
- 1 cup of shredded fresh mozzarella cheese
- ¼ teaspoons of black pepper
- ¼ cup of basil, sliced into thin strips

*you can also use bacon or pancetta slices

Instructions

- Preheat your oven to 350 degrees. If you have a pizza stone, you may place the stone in the oven to heat up.

- Prepare the dough by sprinkling some cornmeal all over the edges. Sprinkle the rest of the cornmeal onto a baking sheet or your pizza stone.

- Spread the minced garlic all over the dough and sprinkle half of the cheese on top. Arrange the tomatoes on top and sprinkle the basil leaves.

- Add the rest of the cheese and bake for about 10 minutes or until the cheese has melted. Slice and serve.

Vegetarian Burgers

Ingredients

- 1 medium sized zucchini, grated
- 1 potato, grated
- 1 medium carrot, grated
- ¼ cup of onions, minced
- ½ teaspoon of chopped oregano
- 2 egg whites or egg replacer equivalent to 2 eggs

Instructions

- Mix all the ingredients together. Make sure that everything has been incorporated well.

- Form into patties in your desired size and thickness and place in the chiller to firm up.

- Heat a pan with a little bit of cooking oil and fry each patty when firm.

Quick Baked Halibut

Ingredients

- 1 teaspoon of olive oil
- 1 cup medium zucchini, diced
- ½ cup of onion, chopped
- 1 large clove of garlic, grated
- 2 cups of Roma tomatoes, diced
- 2 tablespoons of basil, chopped
- ¼ teaspoon of salt
- ¼ teaspoon of ground black pepper
- 2 halibut steaks
- 1/3 cup of feta cheese, crumbled

Instructions

- Preheat your oven to 450 degrees. Line a baking tray with parchment or baking paper.

- In a medium sauce pan, heat olive oil and sauté the garlic, onions and zucchini. Once the zucchini has soften, turn off the heat and stir in the tomatoes, basil and season with salt and pepper.

- Place the halibut steaks on the baking sheet and top with the sautéed vegetables. Drizzle with a little bit of olive oil and bake for about 15 to 20 minutes.

Cornflake Crusted Chicken with Pineapple Salsa

Ingredients

- Salsa
- 1 cup of chopped fresh pineapple
- 2 tablespoons of fresh cilantro leaves, chopped
- 1 tablespoon of finely chopped red onion
- Chicken
- 1/3 cup of lightly crushed plain corn flakes
- 1 cup panko break crumbs or herbed Italian bread crumbs
- ½ teaspoon of salt
- A pinch of pepper
- 4 large chicken cutlets or chicken breast fillet (skinless)
- 1 ½ teaspoons of canola oil for frying, add more if you are using a non-stick pan

Instructions

- Make the salsa first by combing all the ingredients together. Place in an air tight container and refrigerate.

- Combine cornflakes. Salt, pepper and bread crumbs in a small bowl. You can add other herbs such as cilantro, parsley and even paprika. Coat each cutlet with the cornflake mixture and set aside.

- Chill the chicken cutlets and heat your pan.

- Fry the chicken pieces until golden brown. You may bake the chicken fillets in a 450 degree oven for about 15-20 minutes. Serve in a platter with some pineapple salsa on the side.

Lean and Healthy Meatloaf

Ingredients

- 1 lb turkey breast, minced
- 1 lb of lean beef, minced
- ¼ cup of sun dried tomatoes or about 2 tablespoons of tomato paste
- 1 cup of red onion, diced
- 1 cup bell pepper, finely chopped
- ½ cup of carrot, diced finely
- 1 cup of zucchini, grated
- ¼ cup of chopped parsley
- 2 whole eggs
- ½ teaspoon of fresh thyme
- 4 large cloves of garlic, crushed
- ½ cup of panko bread crumbs
- ¼ cup ground flaxseed
- ¼ teaspoon of pepper, salt
- ¼ cup of organic chicken broth

Instructions

- Preheat your oven to 350 degrees and grease a large loaf pan with baking spray or canola oil. You can line it with parchment paper as well.

- Mix all the ingredients together until well combined.

- Place the mixture in the prepared pan and bake for about 1 ½ to 2 hours. Watch over the meatloaf because it can dry out easily, since you will be using turkey and lean meat. If using meat thermometer, the center of the meatloaf should be within the 150 to about 170 degrees.

- Let the cooked meatloaf rest and cool off a bit before unmolding and slicing.

Szechwan Shrimps

Ingredients

- 12 ounces of medium shrimps – peeled, deveined and butterflied
- 4 cloves of garlic, chopped
- ¼ cup chopped green onions
- ¼ teaspoon ginger powder
- 1 tablespoon of ground nut oil/ peanut oil
- ½ teaspoon of red pepper flakes
- 2 tablespoons of ketchup
- 4 tablespoons of water
- 1 tablespoon of tamari or light soy sauce
- 1 teaspoon of honey or agave
- 2 teaspoons of cornstarch

Instructions

- Prepare the sauce by mixing all the wet ingredients together. Add in the red pepper flakes, cornstarch and ground ginger and stir well.

- In a large wok, heat oil and sauté the garlic and green onions until fragrant. Add the shrimps and cook until they are almost cooked and immediately stir in the sauce mixture.

- Wait until the shrimps are fully cooked and the sauce has thickened before turning off the heat. Serve with cooked brown rice.

Cumin and Coriander Crusted Steak

Ingredients

- 1 tablespoon of brown sugar, packed
- 1.2 teaspoon of salt
- ½ teaspoon of pepper
- ½ teaspoon of cumin powder
- ½ teaspoon of coriander powder
- ¼ teaspoon of red pepper powder
- 1 lb boneless sirloin steak

Instructions

- Preheat your oven to 450 degrees. Coat a thick oven safe pan or cast iron skillet with oil and place it inside the oven to heat up.

- Combine all the ingredients together and rub all over the prepared steak.

- Place the steak in the pan and bake for about 7 minutes for medium cook. Slice thinly, against the grain.

Hawaiian Chicken

Ingredients

- 2 pieces of large chicken breast fillet
- ¼ teaspoon each of the following spices:
  - Ginger
  - Paprika
- ¾ teaspoon of onion powder
- 1 ½ teaspoon of garlic powder
- 1 tablespoon of apple cider vinegar
- ¼ cup of tomato sauce
- 1 tablespoon of soy sauce or tamari
- 1 5 ounce can of crushed pineapple
- ½ tablespoon of brown sugar
- Cooked brown rice

Instructions

- Preheat your oven to about 400 degrees and line a baking sheet with parchment paper.

- Place the chicken fillets in the pan and set aside.

- Mix together the onion, garlic, paprika and ginger powders and add in the vinegar. Baste the top of the chicken with the mixture and bake for about 10 minutes.

- After 10 minutes, turn the chicken and baste the top with the remaining vinegar mixture and place it back in the oven.

- In a small bowl, mix the remaining ingredients together except the brown rice. Coat the chicken fillets with the ketchup and pineapple mixture and bake for another 15 minutes or until the chicken fillets have formed crusts.

- Serve on top of a plate of cooked brown rice.

Healthy Chickpea Curry

Ingredients

- 2 cans or 2 cups of cooked garbanzo beans or chickpeas
- 2 T of vegetable oil
- 2 red onions, chopped
- 2 large cloves of garlic, crushed
- 2 teaspoons of fresh ginger, grated
- 6 whole cloves
- 2 sticks of cinnamon
- 1 teaspoon of ground cumin
- 1 teaspoon of ground coriander
- Salt to taste
- 1 teaspoon of cayenne pepper
- 1 teaspoon of turmeric powder
- 1 cup of chopped cilantro
- ½ cup Vegetable stock

Instructions

- Heat oil in the pan and saute all your aromatics (garlic, onions and ginger) until fragrant. Add in your spices and fry the mixture until you can smell all the spices.

- Stir in the garbanzo beans and saute for about 5 minutes.

- Add the stock and simmer for 10 to 15 minutes. Adjust seasoning to taste. Top with fresh cilantro leaves.

All-Spice Pork Chops with Mango Salsa

Ingredients

- ¾ teaspoon of chili powder
- ¼ teaspoon of sea salt
- 1/8 teaspoon of all spice powder
- 4 medium sized pork chops (de-boned)
- 1 and a half cups of diced mangoes (ripe)
- 2 tablespoons of fresh mint, chopped
- 1 tablespoons of lemon juice (fresh)
- 2 teaspoons of sugar
- ¼ teaspoons of red pepper flakes

Instructions

- Prepare the marinade for the pork. Mix together the all spice powder, salt and chili powder. Evenly coat the pork with the spice blend and chill for about 20 minutes.

- Heat a skillet and add oil. Once the chops are ready, pan fry each chop, about 4 to 5 minutes per side or until cooked evenly.

- While waiting for the pork to cook, prepare your salsa by combining the rest of the ingredients. Chill the mango salsa.

- Place 2 pieces of chops per plate and top with mango salsa to serve.

Tomato and Spinach Angel Hair Pasta

Ingredients

- 1 cup of vegetable stock
- 12 pieces of sundried tomatoes
- 2 tablespoons of toasted pine nuts
- ¼ teaspoon of crushed red pepper flakes
- 1 large clove of garlic, crushed
- 1 bunch of fresh spinach leaves, torn into bite size pieces.
- ¼ cup parmesan cheese, grated
- 8 ounces of angel hair pasta, cooked according to package direction
- Salt and pepper to taste

Instructions

- In a large sauce pan, sauté garlic and red pepper flakes until fragrant. Add in the spinach and sun dried tomatoes and cook until the tomatoes have soften. Pour the broth and simmer for about 4 minutes.

- Add the cooked pasta, toss in the pine nuts and simmer until the pasta has absorbed the sauce. Mix well and serve. Sprinkle with parmesan cheese.

Clean, Healthy and Scrumptious Desserts and Snacks

Healthy and Light Frozen Peanut Butter Yogurt

Ingredients

- 2 cups of plain or vanilla flavored yogurt – none or low fat yogurt works too!
- ½ cup milk (dairy or non-dairy)
- ½ cup peanut butter or any nut butter of your choice
- 1 ½ teaspoon of pure vanilla extract
- ¼ teaspoon of sea salt
- 1/3 cup of natural sugar (agave/maple)

Instructions

- In a food processor or blender, mix together all the ingredients until thoroughly combined.

- Place in individual cups, ramekins or air tight containers and freeze. Top with crushed cacao nibs, crushed peanut butter cups or cookies before serving.

Date and Oatmeal Cookies

Ingredients

- 2 large ripe bananas
- 5 large Medjool pitted dates
- 2 cups of rolled oats – gluten free
- Pinch of cinnamon and sea salt

Instructions

- Preheat your oven to 350 degrees and line a baking pan with parchment or baking paper.

- Using a food processor, blend the oats until it reaches a coarse texture. Add in the dates and blend. Add the bananas and the rest of the ingredients to form a dough.

- Scoop out the dough and make about 1 inch balls. Place them evenly on the prepared tray and bake for about 17 minutes. Let the cookies cool before serving.

Non-Dairy Avocado Ice Cream Tropicale

Ingredients

- 2 large ripe avocados, pitted and sliced
- 1 can (15 ounces) pineapple bites, reserve the juice
- ½ cup of coconut milk
- 3 Tablespoons Fresh Lime Juice
- A pinch of sea salt
- ½ cup of raw cocoa powder
- ½ coconut oil
- ¼ cup of maple syrup

Instructions

- Spread the avocado and pineapple slices onto a baking sheet and freeze for 3 hours.

- Process the frozen fruits until the mixture forms a smooth paste and then slowly add the lime juice, pineapple juice, coconut milk, salt and vanilla. Place the mixture in an air tight or covered bowl and freeze until needed.

- While waiting for the avocado ice cream to freeze, prepare the chocolate shards or chips.

- Melt the coconut oil (if solid) and add the cocoa powder. Mix well before adding the maple syrup. Pour the mixture in a lined pan and freeze to solidify.

- Run the avocado mixture in your ice cream maker to churn. It may take about 20 minutes.

- Scoop out the ice cream in bowls and garnish with chocolate shards.

No-Bake Healthy Coconut Snow-Balls

Ingredients

- 1 ¾ cups unsweetened coconut shreds, divided plus a little bit of extra
- 2 teaspoons coconut oil, melted
- 3 tablespoons of maple syrup
- ½ teaspoon vanilla
- ½ teaspoon cinnamon powder
- 1/8 teaspoon of salt

Instructions

- In a food processor, blend together 1 cup of the coconut shreds and the coconut oil until the mixture turns into a paste.

- Add the maple syrup, vanilla, cinnamon and salt. Once incorporated, mix in the rest of the coconut shreds. The mixture will be doughy but not firm.

- Form the dough into balls and dredge them in the remaining coconut flakes. Chill for about an hour.

Mango-Colada Popsicles

Ingredients

- 2 cups frozen mango (organic)
- ¾ cup unsweetened coconut milk
- 1 cup unsweetened full fat coconut cream/milk
- 1 and half tablespoons of honey or agave or coconut nectar for vegans

Instructions

- Puree the frozen mango and add about ¼ cup of the unsweetened coconut milk.

- In a small bowl, add the rest of the coconut milk, 1 cup of the canned coconut cream and your chosen sweetener.

- Prepare your Popsicle molds. Pour 2 tablespoons of mango puree into the molds, let it set for a bit and pour the creamy mixture on top. Cover the molds and insert the sticks. Freeze solid.

Raw Brownies

Ingredients

- 1 cup raw pecans or walnuts
- 1 cup Medjool dates, pitted
- 5 tablespoons of raw cacao or raw cocoa powder
- 2 tablespoons of agave nectar, maple syrup or honey
- ¼ teaspoon sea salt

Instructions

- In a food processor, grind the pecans until it becomes coarse, add the dates. As soon as the mixture becomes sticky, it is now ready for the rest of the ingredients.

- Blend the rest of the ingredients and pour the mixture in a lined baking sheet. Spread evenly and refrigerate for at least 3 hours.

Melon and Apple Granita

Ingredients

- 4 cups of ripe melon, cubed
- 1 cup unsweetened apple juice (bottled or fresh)
- ¼ cup fresh lime juice
- 1 cup blueberries (fresh)
- 1 cup raspberries (fresh)
- Mint leaves for garnish

Instructions

- Blend all ingredients together (except the mint leaves) and pour the liquid mixture into a shallow pan.

- Place the pan in the freezer and let the mixture set for about 3 to 4 hours. Take the pan out and scrape the slightly frozen mixture. Place it back in the freezer.

- Do it again after an hour and let it freeze again. Take the granita out 30 minutes before serving. Scoop the granite into cups and garnish with mint leaves.

Healthy Peachy Green Smoothie

Ingredients

- 2 cups of frozen peaches (if using fresh, freeze them first for about 4 hours)
- 2 cups of spinach leaves
- 1 cup of water
- 1 tablespoon of grated fresh ginger
- 1 tablespoon of honey or agave

Instructions

- Pour water, honey, ginger and spinach in a blender and pulse. The mixture should be smooth and really green.

- Add the frozen peaches and blend until it forms a smoothie-like consistency.

- Serve in chilled tall glasses.

Super Healthy Vegan Nutella

Ingredients

- 2 cups of raw hazelnuts
- 1 ½ cups of melted dark chocolate
- 1/3 cup raw coconut sugar
- 1 tablespoon coconut oil
- 1 teaspoons of vanilla extract
- ¾ teaspoon of salt

Instructions

- Blend the raw hazelnuts into a fine paste and add the rest of the ingredients.

- Store the prepared hazelnut spread in a jar and store in the fridge.

Banana Pudding Pots

Ingredients

- 10 pieces of raw almonds- roasted
- 2 tablespoons of cornstarch
- a pinch of salt
- 3 tablespoons of raw coconut or palm sugar
- 1 beaten egg yolk
- ¾ cup of milk (dairy or non-dairy)
- ½ teaspoon of vanilla extract
- 2 ripe bananas, sliced thinly
- 6 dessert cups

Instructions

- In a food processor, grind the almonds and set aside.

- In a small pot, mix together sugar, cornstarch and salt. Add the egg yolk and slowly pour the milk. Heat the mixture until it thickens.

- Remove the pan from the heat and add the vanilla. Let it cool slightly.

- Prepare the cups by placing a layer of the sliced bananas, topped with the custard cream mixture. Create another layer of bananas and cream until the entire cup has been filled. Sprinkle the chopped almonds. You can choose to serve them cold or warm.

Sugar Free Chocolate Covered Strawberries (Paleo)

Ingredients

- ½ kilos of fresh strawberries, cleaned and patted dry
- 1/3 cup of pure cacao powder
- 1 teaspoon of vanilla bean paste
- A pinch of salt and a teaspoon of honey
- 3 tablespoons of coconut oil, melted

Instructions

- Line a baking sheet with parchment paper.

- In a small bowl, combine cocoa powder, vanilla bean paste, melted coconut oil, salt and honey.

- Dip each strawberry into the chocolate mixture and place on the parchment lined pan.

- Chill or let it set in room temperature.

Conclusion

Clean eating is not that difficult to follow, with all these amazing recipes, tips and guidelines, the only thing that you are left to do is to put everything that you have learned here into action. And once you have gotten used to this really simple, healthy and clean lifestyle, you will be able to achieve that energized and fit body that you have always wanted.

This book hopes that you will keep all the principles mentioned here in mind – from choosing to buy unprocessed whole foods, to cutting back on your sugar intake – because at the end of the day, your main goal is not just to lose those extra pounds, but to also influence and encourage others to take on the clean eating lifestyle.

Finally, if you enjoyed this book, then I'd like to ask you for a big favor, would you be kind enough to leave a review for this book on Amazon? It'd be greatly appreciated!

I wish you the best of luck and enjoy your new clean eating recipes!

Eric Deen

Book 4
My Spiralized Cookbook:
40 Delicious Spiralized
Recipes for Optimum Health,
Weight loss & Wellness You
Need To Know

Introduction

Do you want to learn 40 healthy and delicious spiralized recipes for weight loss and optimum health?

If you are looking for healthy new recipes that not only offer you good foods with health benefits but also look appealing to the eye with the way they are presented you should really enjoy delving into this cookbook.

For those who are looking to try something different in how they prepare and serve their meals you will enjoy trying the great recipes offered in this cookbook. It can get boring sometimes having the same old same old kind of meals. Perhaps you are trying to find a way to keep your family interested in eating healthier food choices. If you can present them with a new meal based on a spiral slicer recipe then I am sure they will be delighted with the presentation and the taste of the meal. It can be trying at times to get your loved ones to eat healthier foods but just keep in mind that you must show your children by example. You are the one that is in control of what foods come into your household.

Sit down and talk with your family and explain to them that you want to present healthier meals to them because you love and care about them and want them to be healthy and strong. You will be surprised how understanding your children can be when you explain the health concerns you have when choosing certain kinds of foods. They will be more willing to except new foods if you explain to them the benefits that these new healthy foods will provide for them. Educating your children on making healthy food choices and what they consist of will make it easier for you to get them on board with a healthier diet plan. I hope you and your family enjoy the spiral slicer recipes gathered in this cookbook!

Chapter 1- Finding the Right Spiral Slicer Tool for You

I must confess I am someone that loves my kitchen gadgets, so I was immediately drawn when I started to see spiral vegetable slicers, spiral cutters, or whatever else you want to call them—I was hooked, I knew I wanted one of those. I am trying to offer my family healthier food choices so when I thought that I could get more vegetables into my family's diet I was attracted to this notion. If I could present more healthy foods to my family in a new way then why not?

To be honest for me the thought of adding more cups full of broccoli to my daily diet did not appeal to me, but if I could add more veggies into my families diet by replacing pasta with vegetables and making them into more tasty side dishes or entrees was something I was going to check out and give it a try.

All of the Julienne and spiral slicer peelers all

appeared to have fun varieties of spiral slices that you could make. The Mandoline even offered an array of cuts that I could use in making my vegetable dishes with. I now had a goal or mission if you will to find a spiral cutter that would suit my needs best. I was on the search for this gadget that would help me to reduce the carbohydrates in my family's diet.

I found the one that would work for me—more about my choice of spiral slicer later. I began to do some experimenting. Most of the recipes I tried at first were designed to substitute pastas in a dish with zucchini noodles. They were really easy and quick to make and they tasted great—my family loved them!

I wanted to find other ways to use my newly acquired kitchen gadget. So I decided I was going to liven up a salad. I began thinking what if I could use favorite classic dishes but just give them a bit of an upgrade in the presentation department by using spiral veggies in them.

I began to realize that there was a lot more I could do with my new gadget than I had originally realized. I started to try different combinations of fruits and veggies some were more favored than others. But in the process I ended up coming up with side dishes, main dishes that I wanted to share with others. I served my dishes to friends and family asking their honest opinions of the dishes so I ended up with the best of the best now gathered here in these pages. I was sure my husband might grumble a bit when I made some changes to some of his favorite meals but to my surprise he enjoyed the new versions. He was also happy because they were healthier as he wants to eat better to help control his diabetes.

So here in this cookbook is my own collection of my favorite spiral veggie dishes and those of my loved ones too! In this cookbook my goal was to bring together new recipes for main dishes, salads, soups, and side dishes that are a more healthier and appealing choice in order to help us to eat more vegetables. Included are dishes for vegetarians, low carbohydrate diets, gluten-free diets, also a good variety of fish, meat, and poultry dishes too.

There is recipes that will make great side dishes and salads that will go with any type of meal that you are serving. Learning to expand the traditional boundaries of vegetables is going to make your options on preparing your meals so much more allowing you to serve in so many different ways!

You are going to find that a spiral slicer is going to add so much more to your experience of eating fruits and vegetables, this cookbook will help to guide you through ways that you can present your family with meals that are healthy and can be prepared quickly. But most of all you will please your friends and family with the great tastes of your meals. Enjoy exploring the world of spiralizing your foods!

If you are trying to find a more tantalizing way to serve your fruits and vegetables then you are ready to give spiralizing a try. You are going to be creating meals that are healthy, quick to prepare but most of all are great tasting! You can use a spiral cutter to cut your veggies and fruits for soups, salads, main dishes, and sides much quicker.

Cutting long slices are appealing for a healthy alternative to pasta. The shapes are also ideal for soups, salads, stir fries, and side dishes. You can also use your spiral cutter to make garnishes for your appetizers and many other dishes.

Spiral slicers, Julienne Peelers, Mandolines, Spiral Slicers, and other Veggie Cutters. Each of these are used to cut veggies and fruit into thin, long, slices that are extremely stream lined.

There is a vast number of *Spiral Slicers* in the market today to choose from. You can find them in kitchen stores, or big retail stores, Amazon, etc.

There is basically three different types of spiral slicers and amongst these are many brand names.

Spiral slicer is the first type it is the biggest or largest. It features three to four different sizes of cutting blades. You are able to cut from spaghetti size noodles, to fettuccine, to wider egg noodle sized pasta.

Advantages: It has a large base with suction cups that hold to your cupboard; it has a hand crank that keeps your fingers away from the blades it also gives you more leverage for turning denser veggies.

Disadvantages: This is a large gadget due to its overall size if you have limited kitchen space this would not be a good choice. Some of the models have platforms extending beyond the blades while others do not. It is nice to have this so that your veggies you are cutting can drop right into bowl meaning less cleanup for you. You need to take caution when changing the blades or cleaning them.

Midsize Spiral slicer is the second type. It usually has four different size cutting blades. It is more compact than the previous type.

Small Spiral slicer is the third type it is a handheld kitchen tool. It has two blades one for thick pasta another for thin pasta. This is a good choice if you only want to use it to make spaghetti sized noodles. It is a good compact tool for this purpose.

Julienne Peelers these are kitchen tools that have been around for a very long time. You can find these at most stores that sell small kitchen gadgets. They come with various blades on different brands and types. Make sure you choose one that has ultra-sharp serrated blades that will be ideal for the types of size cuts that you want to make. These are small enough that you can keep them in a utensil drawer.

Mandolines are another kitchen tool that have been around for a long time. They too can be found at most stores that sell small kitchen gadgets. These are really good to use if you are cutting eggplant into wide lasagna noodle size slices. Look for a Mandoline that offers multiple size blades and a thickness adjuster. Make sure that it has a food holder and protects your fingers from being cut. You can also find Mandolines that have clamps on them so you can secure them to the side of a bowl.

Other Spiral Vegetable Cutters. If you have a food processor or a stand mixer with the ability to add attachments you can also use these appliances to cut your veggies and fruits. There is attachments that can do shredding, grinding, and julienne cuts. Depending on the spiral slicer that you choose will have an effect on what your choices are for spiral sizes.

Garlic Press: A garlic press is not a necessity but you will find they are handy to have when you need to mince some garlic they do the job well. They are also much easier to use than a knife for this job.

Strainer: It is good to have a strainer in your kitchen especially when you are using a lot of foods that need to be washed before use, and also strained of excess water. You can also use some paper towel to help you to get rid of any excess water if you want to speed the process along.

Vegetable Peeler: It will really help you when you need to peel your veggies and fruit it just makes this process so much easier when preparing the foods.

Large Sharp Knife: You need a good large sharp knife to help you to cut up denser larger veggies and it well help to cut the ends off your produce.

Chapter 2:
Stocking Up On Spiralizing Supplies

The great thing about adding more veggies to your diet is you are going to be trading in the traditional pasta for your spiralizing veggies that is going to eliminate gluten, lower your calories, and reduce your intake of carbohydrates.

Vegetables & Fruits

Make sure to use good quality and freshest produce that you can find. You want to make sure that your meals are going to be the best they can be so strive for quality foods to be included in your meals. Fully ripened fruits and vegetables should always be used when preparing your meals. You do not want to use produce that is either over-ripe or under-ripe. By choosing produce that is in season in your area you will get best results from this choice. Not only will they taste better if grown locally but they often are sold at very good prices especially at the local farmer's markets. Zucchini is a very popular choice of veggie amongst those that like to spiralize their meals. It is the most popular choice to substitute pasta in recipes. But there is also many other choices you can try to make delicious healthy meals for your family. I find some of the best veggies to spiralize are: zucchini, sweet potatoes, summer squash, cucumbers, carrots, russet potatoes, eggplant, cabbage, beets turnips, parsnips, onions, radishes. Fruits that are ideal are apples and pears.

Condiments & Broths

Using beef, chicken, or vegetable broths are wonderful for simmering veggie noodles in. Broths will add a nice deep flavor to your meats and soups. You can buy containers of broth, bouillon cubes, or make it from scratch.

Having a variety of condiments will help to add some zing to your flavoring of your meals try using: honey, Worcestershire sauce, and Dijon Mustard, honey mustard. These items will certainly come in handy when you are preparing your meals they will help to give the flavor of your meals a nice boost.

Oils & Vinegars

Using oil is one of the standard ingredients for many of these recipes you can choose from the best oils that I would suggest are extra virgin olive oil and coconut oil. Vinegar is a great staple to have on hand you will be able to use this in many of your meals. There is an assortment of different vinegars to choose from my personal favorite is apple cider vinegar.

Herbs & Seasoning

When you are adding dried herbs and seasoning to your meals remember that a small amount will go a long way in flavoring your foods. Make sure to follow the guidelines in the recipes for the amounts to use so that you get the proper consistency and flavor. You may want to adjust the amounts to your personal taste once you become familiar with making the recipes you can tweak them to suit your tastes.

Ingredients List

Make sure that when you are planning to make a certain recipe that you write a list of the ingredients that are needed before you go shopping, then make sure to bring your list. I myself am great at writing lists but when

I get to the grocery store I often realize I have forgotten my list. Before leaving the house give yourself a check over to make sure you have your shopping supplies such as list and shopping bags. When you are using fresh fruits and veggies in a recipe you should buy them when you want to make the dish or no more than two to three days previous to preparing dish for the best results. Make sure to have your veggies prepped and ready before you begin to cook so that you are not left with foods that are overcooked and soggy. Add your ingredients in the order that they are listed within the recipe directions.

Tips for Best Results

You should make sure to read the manual that you will receive with your spiral slicer so that you assemble it properly and know the most effective way to use it. Try and choose thick, firm, and straight veggies and fruits. Do not choose veggies that are too big as they will be hard for you to handle and they may not fit into your spiral slicer. Try and use veggies that have little to no seeds in them. If they are a veggie that does have seeds pick the thinner ones as they will have less seeds. Make sure you are using good quality produce and wash and dry them properly before using. When putting into your spiral slicer make sure they are as straight as you can place them. When you are cooking veggies it is better if you do not overcrowd the pot or pan you are cooking in. Clean your tools right after using to keep them in the best condition.

Safety Tips

The blades are very sharp on these slicers so take extra care when washing and handling them. Make sure that you dry your blades after washing to prevent them from tarnishing or rusting. Now it is time to begin using your spiral slicer and getting creative in the kitchen in a healthy way!

Chapter 3:
Spiralized Salads

To begin your adventure into the world of spiral slicer meals here is a wide variety of soups and salad recipes I am sure you are going to enjoy preparing these healthy fun dishes!

1. Thai Salad & Peanut Lime Ginger Dressing

Servings: 4
Ingredients:

- three tablespoons of fresh cilantro
- one lime wedge
- two and a half tablespoons of unsalted peanuts
- one English cucumber, sliced
- one quarter cup of finely shredded fresh ginger
- two yellow beets, spiralized
- two large carrots, spiralized
- one cup of Napa cabbage chopped
- four tablespoons of Peanut Lime Ginger Dressing

Peanut Ginger Dressing Ingredients:

- half a cup of extra virgin olive oil
- one tablespoon of Stevia
- two tablespoons of coconut milk
- one quarter cup of shredded fresh ginger
- one tablespoon of apple cider vinegar
- two tablespoons of lime juice
- two tablespoons of peanut butter smooth

- two tablespoons of cilantro
- one teaspoon of minced garlic

Directions for Dressing:

In a blender puree all of the ingredients except for the olive oil. When blender is running add the oil in an easy stream until the dressing is nice and smooth.

Directions:

Put the cabbage in a large serving bowl. Using either a julienne or a spiral slicer, spiralize the yellow beets, and carrots into spaghetti size noodles. Add these to the top of the cabbage. Drizzle on top with Peanut Ginger Dressing. Add peanuts, cilantro, cucumbers, and lime as garnish and enjoy!

2. Kohlrabi Salad

Servings: 4

Ingredients:

- two tablespoons of balsamic dressing
- one tablespoon of dried cranberries
- one green apple, spiralized
- two tablespoons of walnuts chopped
- one kohlrabi peeled and spiralized
- two cups of baby arugula
- one cup of diced feta cheese
- garnish with sesame seeds

Directions:

Place the arugula in a large bowl, using either a julienne peeler or a spiral slicer to spiralize the kohlrabi and the green apple into spaghetti size strands. Add these to the top of the arugula. Then add diced feta cheese, dried cranberries, walnuts and dressing. Then garnish with sesame seeds and serve.

3. Tomatoes & Mango with Curry Zucchini Pasta

Servings: 2
Ingredients:

- half a mango cut into cubes
- six cherry tomatoes cut in half
- one zucchini, spiralized
- two tablespoons of extra virgin olive oil
- two cups of baby spinach
- one tablespoon of fresh basil chopped
- two tablespoons of curry powder
- sea salt
- fresh parsley for garnish
- slivered almonds for garnish

Directions:

Using a spiral slicer or julienne peeler, spiralize the zucchini into spaghetti size noodles in a bowl. Add the sea salt, olive oil, basil, and curry powder to zucchini. Toss gently and then set aside.

On a plate add baby spinach, tomatoes, and mango, top with zucchini mixture then add parsley and almonds as garnish.

4. Asian Sweet Potato Salad

Servings: 4
Ingredients:

- eight green onions finely sliced
- two tablespoons of sesame seeds
- two cups of kale remove the stems
- one red bell pepper thinly sliced
- five ounces of portabella mushrooms thinly sliced
- two tablespoons of sugar-free maple syrup
- one yellow onion thinly sliced
- one quarter cup of tamari sauce or low-sodium soy sauce
- three and a half tablespoons of extra virgin olive oil divided
- three large carrots, spiralized
- two large sweet potatoes peeled and spiralized
- one teaspoon of minced garlic

Directions:

Using a julienne peeler or a spiral slicer, spiralize the sweet potatoes into spaghetti size noodles. Spiralize you carrots cut into four to four and a half inch lengths and set aside. In a deep skillet toss around sweet potato noodles with two teaspoons of oil cooking over medium-low heat until slightly softened. Remove noodles from heat. In a small bowl combine the soy sauce, maple syrup, garlic and two tablespoons of oil. Blend this well. Add to the pan with the sweet potatoes and gently toss. Remove to serving plate and add sesame seeds and green onions.

5. Bitter Sweet Cucumber Salad

Servings: 4
Ingredients:

- half of a red onion sliced and quartered
- three English cucumbers, spiralized
- three quarter cup of apple cider vinegar
- one and a half tablespoons of Stevia
- one tablespoon of sesame seeds
- fresh parsley finely chopped for garnish

Directions:

Spiralize your cucumbers into wide noodles using either a julienne peeler or a spiral slicer. Collect the noodles into a bowl. Add vinegar, red onion, Stevia and one quarter cup of water. Cover the bowl tightly and refrigerate the noodles for at least two hours stir occasionally. One the salad is well chilled then top with sesame seeds and parsley.

6. Curried White Kidney Beans & Zucchini Salad

Servings: 4
Ingredients:

- two zucchini, spiralized
- two large carrots, spiralized
- one green cabbage cut into thin strips
- one can of white kidney beans drained and rinsed
- one quarter cup of fresh cilantro chopped
- four green onions sliced
- one red bell pepper thinly sliced
- pinch of red chili flakes
- pinch of fresh ground pepper
- pinch of sea salt
- one third cup of tahini
- three tablespoons of lime juice
- four tablespoons of sugar-free maple syrup
- one tablespoon of ground ginger
- one tablespoon of curry powder

Directions:
In a large bowl add ground ginger, maple syrup, curry powder, lime juice, and tahini. Mix these ingredients well add a bit of water if needed. Using a spiral slicer or julienne peeler spiralize your zucchini, and carrots into

spaghetti size noodles. In a large bowl, add cabbage, bell pepper, noodles, green onions, cilantro, and white kidney beans. Add your dressing and toss to coat. You can season with red chili flakes and salt and pepper.

7. Apple, Beet, & Radish Slaw

Servings: 4
Ingredients:

- one red beet, spiralized
- one bunch of radishes, spiralized
- one green medium sized apple, spiralized
- one quarter cup of apple cider vinegar
- Romaine lettuce leaves
- pinch of sea salt
- two teaspoons of finely grated orange zest
- two tablespoons of fresh ginger finely grated
- one teaspoon of basil
- one quarter cup of cilantro
- two tablespoons of low-sodium soy sauce

Directions:

Spiralize your apple, beet, and radishes into spaghetti sized noodles using a julienne peeler or a spiral slicer. Add these ingredients to a large bowl along with vinegar, soy sauce, cilantro, basil, ginger, and orange zest. Toss your salad add a pinch of sea salt if you desire then allow it to rest for five minutes before serving. Place Romaine leaves on top of plates then put the slaw on top of them and serve.

8. Sweet Potato Walnut Salad

Servings: 4
Ingredients:

- three sweet potatoes peeled and spiralized
- half a cup of extra virgin olive oil divided
- sea salt
- half a cup of scallions chopped
- two tablespoons of apple cider vinegar
- one teaspoon of Dijon Mustard
- one teaspoon of minced garlic
- half a cup of feta cheese crumbled
- one bunch of baby spinach leaves
- half a cup of walnuts chopped

Directions:

Preheat your oven to 425 degrees Fahrenheit. Using a spiral slicer or julienne peeler spiralize your sweet potatoes into spaghetti size noodles. Toss in two tablespoons of oil with your sweet potatoes and sea salt. Place on a large roasting pan and cover with foil. Roast for about 15 minutes or until golden brown and turn occasionally. During the last five minutes put your walnuts on a small baking sheet and add them to the oven. Put your spinach into a large bowl with feta cheese, and scallions. Put the remaining olive oil, mustard, vinegar, garlic into jar and shake well to mix and blend ingredients. Pour this over your spinach mixture then add the potatoes and walnuts on top and serve.

9. Spicy Cucumber Salad

Servings: 6
Ingredients:

- four cucumbers, spiralized
- two carrots, spiralized
- one teaspoon of garlic minced
- one teaspoon of fresh ginger grated
- one teaspoon of raw honey
- half a tablespoon of apple cider vinegar
- one tablespoon of extra virgin olive oil
- one quarter cup of low-sodium soy sauce
- sesame seeds to garnish
- cilantro for garnish
- cayenne pepper sauce for spice level you want

Directions:

Spiralize your carrots and zucchini into spaghetti size noodles then place the noodles into a bowl. In a mixing bowl whisk together the lime juice, honey, ginger, oil, vinegar, and cayenne pepper sauce. Add the dressing to the noodles and toss gently adding cilantro to garnish and sesame seeds.

10. Zucchini & Dandelion Salad

Servings: 6
Ingredients:

- two zucchini, spiralized
- four cups of Dandelion leaves
- one cup of cherry tomatoes halved
- one teaspoon of extra virgin olive oil
- two tablespoons of balsamic vinaigrette
- sea salt
- fresh ground pepper
- half a cup of feta cheese crumbled
- four tablespoons of slivered almonds for garnish

Directions:

Spiralize your zucchini into spaghetti size noodles using a spiral slicer or julienne peeler. Add the Dandelion leaves, feta cheese, olive oil, balsamic vinaigrette. Sprinkle on top with slivered almonds and serve.

10. Zucchini & Dandelion Salad

Servings: 6
Ingredients:

- two zucchini, spiralized
- four cups of Dandelion leaves
- one cup of cherry tomatoes halved
- one teaspoon of extra virgin olive oil
- two tablespoons of balsamic vinaigrette
- sea salt
- fresh ground pepper
- half a cup of feta cheese crumbled
- four tablespoons of slivered almonds for garnish

Directions:

Spiralize your zucchini into spaghetti size noodles using a spiral slicer or julienne peeler. Add the Dandelion leaves, feta cheese, olive oil, balsamic vinaigrette. Sprinkle on top with slivered almonds and serve.

11. Tomatoes, Carrots & Zucchini Salad

Servings: 4
Ingredients:

- one quarter cup of apple cider vinegar
- quarter cup of grape tomatoes halved
- one quarter cup of coconut oil melted
- one teaspoon of minced garlic
- one teaspoon of Stevia
- half a teaspoon of sea salt
- two zucchini, spiralized
- one large carrot, spiralized
- two tablespoons of fresh basil chopped
- half a cup of Parmesan cheese shaved

Directions:

Spiralize your carrot and zucchini into spaghetti size noodles using a spiral slicer or julienne peeler. In a bowl combine carrot, zucchini, and tomatoes. In a container with lid combine oil, vinegar, garlic, Stevia, garlic seal with lid and shake well. Pour the dressing over the noodles and toss lightly then allow it to sit for ten minutes, add Parmesan and basil then, serve.

12. Spicy Mango & Cucumber Salad

Servings: 4
Ingredients:

- three cucumbers, spiralized
- two tablespoons of extra virgin olive oil
- sea salt
- two cups of kale greens
- half a mango cubed
- two tablespoons of curry powder
- fresh chopped cilantro
- two tablespoons of slivered almonds

Directions:

Spiralize your cucumbers into spaghetti size noodles into a bowl using a spiral slicer or a julienne peeler. Add oil, cilantro, and sea salt to cucumber. Add the amount of curry powder that you personally would like for the spice level that you prefer. Toss lightly then set aside. On a serving plate Place kale greens then tomatoes and mango on top. Then put your cucumber mixture on top and sprinkle with slivered almonds.

13. Greek Cucumber Salad

Servings: 2
Ingredients:

- one English cucumber, spiralized
- one tablespoon of red onion thinly sliced
- ten black olives pitted
- half a fresh lemon
- half a cup of feta cheese crumbled
- one tablespoon of fresh oregano leaves minced
- half a cup of cherry tomatoes halved
- one red bell pepper thinly sliced
- half a tablespoon of extra virgin olive oil
- sea salt
- fresh ground pepper to taste

Directions:

Using a spiral slicer or a julienne peeler spiralize your cucumber to about the size of fettuccine size noodles. Put your cucumber spirals into a large bowl. Add bell pepper, olives, tomatoes, red onion. Squeeze over it the juice of half a lemon. Drizzle with half of the oil. Add the oregano. Toss salad gently until it is evenly coated. Add to a serving plate. Top with feta then drizzle the remaining oil over it and serve.

14. Salad of Many Colors

Servings: 4
Ingredients:

- two English cucumbers, spiralized
- one large beet, spiralized
- two carrots, spiralized
- one mango, julienned
- two tablespoons of salad dressing of your choice I would suggest a nice garlic dressing

Homemade Garlic-Basil Dressing Ingredients:

- one third cup of extra virgin olive oil
- one quarter cup of fresh lime juice
- one quarter cup of fresh basil finely chopped
- one tablespoon of honey
- one teaspoon of garlic
- half a teaspoon of sea salt
- one quarter teaspoon of fresh ground pepper

Directions:
Spiralize your carrots, beet, and cucumber into spaghetti size noodles. Toss with mango and dressing until all is well coated. Let it sit for a few minutes to settle then put into serving bowls and enjoy this yummy dish!

Chapter 4:
Spiralized Poultry Main Dishes

You will find a wind array of main spiral slicer dishes that you and your family will be able to enjoy for many years to come eating your way to health and wellness with these tasty recipes!

Spiralized Poultry Recipes

15. Lemon-Garlic Turkey with Zucchini Noodles

Servings: 4
Ingredients:

- half a pound of turkey breast cut into strips
- half a teaspoon of extra virgin olive oil
- two zucchini, spiralized
- two tablespoons of organic butter
- one tablespoon of parsley, minced
- zest from half a fresh lemon
- one teaspoon of minced garlic
- half a teaspoon of sea salt
- one quarter teaspoon of ground black pepper
- one quarter cup of fresh parsley chopped

Directions:

Mix together in a bowl garlic, oil, parsley, salt, pepper, lemon juice. Add your turkey strips to the bowl and cover and marinate for 30 minutes. Spiralize your zucchini into spaghetti size noodles and set aside. In a skillet heat butter over low heat. Remove your turkey strips from marinade and reserve the marinade. Add your turkey strips to pan and cook for 4 minutes on each side or until they are cooked through and slightly browned on the outside. Add your marinade to the pan and simmer for a few minutes. Add salt and pepper to taste and remove from heat. Put on to serving plates then sprinkle with fresh parsley.

16. Mediterranean Chicken with Artichoke Hearts

Servings: 4
Ingredients:

- four chicken cutlets
- one tablespoon of extra virgin olive oil
- four tablespoons of organic butter
- one tablespoon of coconut flour
- three quarter teaspoon of basil
- half a cup of low-sodium chicken broth
- half a cup of white wine
- one quarter teaspoon of allspice
- one cup of marinated artichoke hearts drained
- eight Greek olives pitted and halved
- two tablespoons of pine nuts
- cayenne pepper sauce to desired level of spicy

Directions:

Heat a large skillet over medium heat with olive oil. Add chicken cutlets and cook for four minutes per side or until your chicken is browned and cooked through. Transfer you chicken to a plate and set aside. In the pan with the drippings add butter heating until melted. Add the chicken broth, wine, and a few drops of cayenne pepper sauce to desired level of spicy. Blend in the allspice, basil, and flour keep stirring until well blended.

Spiralize your zucchini into fettuccine size noodles then add them to the sauce cooking for about three minutes stir gently. Remove noodles from pan. Add your artichoke hearts to the pan mixing in sauce, adding chicken cutlets back into the pan. Toss and combine them with the sauce. Remove them from heat serve over bed of zucchini noodles then top with pine nuts.

17. Spicy Chicken & Peanut Sauce with Summer Squash Noodles

Servings: 6
Ingredients:

- three summer squash, spiralized
- one quarter cup of fresh cilantro
- two zucchini, spiralized
- one teaspoon of minced garlic
- one tablespoon of low-sodium soy sauce
- half a cup of peanut butter creamy
- four tablespoons of apple cider vinegar
- two teaspoons of extra virgin olive oil
- half a teaspoon of Stevia
- five cups of diced chicken breast cooked
- two tablespoons of sesame seeds

Directions:

In a bowl add soy sauce, vinegar, peanut butter, garlic, Stevia, oil and mix until ingredients are well blended. Slowly add about one third cup of water or as much as needed to reach the desired consistency. Spiralize your zucchini, and your summer squash into spaghetti size noodles. Boil zucchini and summer squash for three minutes then drain once vegetables have cooled. Place on serving plate top with chicken mixture then add cilantro and sesame seeds.

18. Turkey Sausage and Rutabaga Noodles

Servings: 4
Ingredients:

- three rutabaga, spiralized
- one tablespoon of organic butter
- three tablespoons of extra virgin olive oil divided
- two small red onions thinly sliced
- four tablespoons of balsamic vinegar
- pinch of sea salt
- ground pepper to taste
- four cooked turkey sausages
- two cups of spinach fresh chopped

Directions:

In a skillet heat butter with one tablespoon of oil over medium heat. Add the onions and saute for 20 minutes or until soft and golden brown. Add the spinach and saute until it is wilted. Add balsamic vinegar, increase the heat to medium-high cooking for two minutes or until the liquid is absorbed. Season with salt and pepper. Spiralize rutabagas into spaghetti size noodles. In another pan heat in remaining two tablespoons of oil over medium heat. On one side of your skillet cook rutabaga then add turkey sausage on the other side cook sausage for five minutes or until well browned. Serve your sausage bedside your rutabaga noodles and pour spinach mixture over.

19. Spiralized Russet Potatoes & Chicken

Servings: 4

Ingredients:

- six tablespoons of organic butter, divided
- four tablespoons of sour cream
- one tablespoon of extra virgin olive oil
- one celery stalk, finely diced
- two cups of low-sodium chicken broth
- four tablespoons of coconut flour
- two tablespoons of paprika
- two white onions, thinly sliced
- one whole chicken, quartered
- four russet potatoes, spiralized

Directions:

In a dutch oven melt three tablespoons of butter on medium-low heat. Stir in the onions and saute them for 15 minutes then remove onions from the pan. Add the remaining three tablespoons of butter and melt in the Dutch oven. Add the chicken. Brown the chicken in the butter turn the chicken often. Add the chicken broth. sauteed onions, and diced celery to the chicken. Cover and simmer for one hour or until the chicken is fully cooked. Spiralize your potatoes make them into egg noodles size. In a skillet heat oil over medium heat then add the noodles and cook for eight minutes. Add your noodles to a serving plate. Remove your chicken from the Dutch oven and place on plate on top of bed of noodles. Add sour cream and flour to the gravy in the pan then pour this over your meal.

20. Chicken & Wine-Mushroom Sauce with Zucchini Noodles

Servings: 4
Ingredients:

- four zucchini, spiralized
- four tablespoons of organic butter
- two chicken breasts boneless, skinless
- one tablespoon of sea salt
- one tablespoon of black pepper
- one teaspoon of garlic minced
- half a cup of finely chopped red onion
- one cup of sliced mushrooms
- half a cup of white wine vinegar
- one third cup of half-and-half cream
- half a cup of almond flour
- chopped fresh parsley for garnish

Directions:

Spiralize your zucchini into spaghetti size noodles pat them dry with a piece of paper towel and set aside. In pan saute half of the butter over medium heat add chicken sprinkle with salt and pepper and cook until the chicken is lightly browned. Remove chicken from pan and cube into small pieces about one inch big. To the pan and drippings add the onion, garlic, mushrooms, thyme, white wine vinegar, half-and-half, flour, stir and simmer for five minutes. Mix the noodles with chicken and sauce then add to a casserole dish and bake for 30 minutes.

Chapter 5:
Spiralized Beef Main Dishes

In this chapter you will find some great tasty spiralized beef dishes that your whole family will enjoy and be asking you to make them not because they are healthy but because they taste so yummy!

21.Kale & Turkey Sausage Eggplant Zucchini Lasagna

Servings: 4
Ingredients:

- two eggplant, peeled and cut into lengthwise slices of eight
- two zucchini, cut lengthwise into six slices
- one quarter cup of coconut oil melted
- four tablespoons of extra virgin olive oil
- sea salt
- fresh ground black pepper
- one teaspoon of garlic
- one onion chopped
- one teaspoon of dried Italian seasoning
- twelve ounces of ground turkey
- one five ounce pack of cheese and garlic croutons, crushed
- two cups of shredded mozzarella cheese
- one egg lightly beaten
- half a cup of grated Parmesan cheese
- one fifteen ounce container of ricotta cheese
- one quarter cup of fresh basil, chopped
- one chunky can of pasta sauce

Directions:

Heat the oven to 425 degrees Fahrenheit. Coat two 15×10×1 inch baking pans with cooking spray. Use a Mandoline slicer to cut the eggplant and zucchini for even slices. Arrange your eggplant and zucchini on the baking sheets. Brush the tops with one quarter cup of olive oil. Season with salt and pepper. Bake for 15 minutes or until tender. Remove from oven. Reduce the temperature to 375 degrees Fahrenheit. In a large skillet heat one tablespoon of coconut oil over medium heat add the ground turkey and cook for eight minutes until it is browned. Add onion and garlic and cook for another five minutes. Stir in the pasta sauce, Italian seasoning, and three tablespoons of basil.

Remove from heat. In bowl mix ricotta cheese, egg, and parmesan cheese until well blended. Coat a 13×9 inch baking dish with cooking spray. Layer half of the eggplant into it. Top eggplant with ricotta mixture, half of the zucchini, and one and a half cups of pasta sauce and one cup of mozzarella. Top with the remaining zucchini, pasta, eggplant and ricotta mixture. Bake for 35 minutes or until hot and cheese is bubbling. Remove from oven. In a small bowl mix crushed croutons with remaining two tablespoons of melted coconut oil. Sprinkle evenly over the top then add the remaining one cup of Mozzarella cheese. Bake for another ten minutes until cheese is melted and croutons are slightly toasted. Remove from oven and let stand for five minutes. Sprinkle with remaining one tablespoon of basil and enjoy!

22. Curried Beef with Sweet Potato Noodles

Servings: 6
Ingredients:

- three tablespoons of coconut oil, melted
- one pound of beef stew, cut into one inch pieces
- pinch of sea salt
- fresh ground pepper to taste
- one large white onion, sliced
- one teaspoon of garlic minced
- one cinnamon stick
- one bay leaf
- two medium tomatoes, quartered
- three tablespoons of chutney
- two zucchini, spiralized
- two yellow squash, spiralized
- three quarter cups of milk
- one quarter teaspoon of dried red pepper
- one teaspoon of fresh lemon juice
- one tablespoon of curry powder
- one tablespoon of ginger minced
- two tablespoons of fresh cilantro, chopped

Directions:
In a large skillet on medium heat, heat one

tablespoon of oil. Add your beef in batches as it makes for easier browning. Season beef with salt and pepper. Sear your beef for about six minutes or until brown on all sides. Add more oil if necessary. With a slotted spoon transfer your beef to a plate. Heat the remaining oil in the same skillet adding onions saute for about five minutes then return the beef to the skillet. Add cinnamon stick, bay leaf, red pepper, garlic and stir. Mix in the milk, tomatoes, lemon juice, ginger, curry powder, and some salt and bring to a boil. Reduce heat to simmer and cover stir occasionally for two hours or until beef is tender. Remove the cover and increase the heat until the juices start to thicken. Spiralize yellow squash, and zucchini into spaghetti size noodles. Add your noodles to the beef mixture and toss gently cooking for another three minutes. Top with cilantro and serve.

23. Turkey Spaghetti Sauce & Zucchini Noodles

Servings: 4
Ingredients:

- one pound of ground turkey
- one yellow onion diced
- one tablespoon of garlic minced
- 28 ounce can of crushed tomatoes
- half a teaspoon of dried oregano
- one teaspoon of dried basil
- 1-26 ounce can of pasta sauce
- two zucchini, spiralized
- two tablespoons of coconut oil, melted
- Parmesan cheese

Directions:

In a large saucepan saute ground turkey over medium heat for ten minutes or until it is browned. Add onions and one tablespoon of oil, saute onion for five minutes. Add garlic, pasta sauce, tomatoes, oregano, and basil, bring to a boil. Lower to a simmer and cover for 45 minutes. Use a spiral slicer to spiralize your zucchini into spaghetti size noodles. In a different pan add remaining oil and saute the zucchini for about five minutes. Put zucchini noodles on serving plates then top with sauce and garnish with Parmesan then serve.

24. Garlic Pork Chops & Applesauce with Zucchini Noodles

Servings: 2
Ingredients:

- two zucchini, spiralized
- two pork chops
- one serving of unsweetened applesauce
- dash of cinnamon
- 1-28 ounce can of diced tomatoes, drained
- four tablespoons of balsamic dressing
- two tablespoons of fresh basil, chopped
- black pepper to taste
- garlic powder
- one teaspoon of minced garlic
- fresh parsley, chopped for garnish

Directions:

Heat oven to 375 degrees Fahrenheit. Spray a baking sheet place your pork chops on baking sheet and sprinkle with garlic powder lightly on both sides. Bake for 20 minutes then flip over and bake for another 20 minutes or until both sides are golden brown. Add a tablespoon or so of applesauce on top of pork chops in the last five minutes of baking and add sprinkle of cinnamon. Put bake into oven to finish baking. Spiralize your zucchini into spaghetti size noodles. In a small pan put tomatoes, minced garlic, basil, and balsamic dressing. Put up to medium-low heat and add zucchini noodles and stir lightly cooking for another five minutes. Take pork chops and put on serving plates and add the zucchini noodles on the side garnish with parsley and enjoy!

25. Alfredo Pasta with Asparagus & Mushrooms

Servings: 2
Ingredients:

- two zucchini, spiralized
- two tablespoons of extra virgin olive oil
- five ounces of sliced mushrooms
- half a cup of red bell pepper, thinly sliced
- one cup of asparagus, chopped
- one bottle of store bought Alfredo sauce
- add black pepper to taste
- two ounces of prosciutto, chopped

Directions:

Spiralize your zucchini into spaghetti size noodles. Set aside. In a frying pan add the oil, asparagus, mushrooms, and prosciutto. Saute until the prosciutto is lightly crispy. Add in the Alfredo sauce and zucchini and toss lightly on simmer for about three minutes. Remove from heat. Serve in pasta bowls and garnish with fresh parsley or basil.

26. Garlic Pork & Zucchini Noodles

Servings: 4
Ingredients:

- one pound of ground pork
- one small red onion, diced
- one red bell pepper, diced
- one teaspoon of garlic, minced
- pinch of black pepper
- pinch of sea salt
- 14 ounce can of coconut milk
- one carrot, spiralized
- two zucchini, spiralized
- half a cup of almond butter
- one quarter cup of low-sodium soy sauce
- two tablespoons of lime juice
- two tablespoons of sriracha

Directions:

Spiralize your carrot, and zucchini into spaghetti size noodles. Set these aside in bowl lined with paper towel. In a frying pan add oil on medium heat and pork, onion, bell pepper, garlic, and salt and pepper. Saute for seven minutes or so or until pork is no longer pink in color. Toss in carrot and cook for another three minutes. Toss in zucchini and cook for another two minutes. Remove from heat and place into serving bowls. In a small saucepan whisk together milk, soy sauce, butter, lime juice, and sriracha cook on low heat for several minutes. Pour the sauce over the noodles and pork in bowls. Sprinkle with chopped cilantro as a garnish.

27. Potato Spaghetti Pie

Servings: 4
Ingredients:

- one sweet potato, spiralized
- two russet potatoes, spiralized
- one tablespoon of organic butter melted
- one egg beaten
- cooking spray
- one quarter cup of Parmesan, grated
- two tablespoons of coconut oil, melted
- half a red onion, chopped
- one teaspoon garlic, minced
- one cup of low-fat cottage cheese, drained
- half a cup of mozzarella cheese, shredded
- eight ounces of ground Italian sausage
- one eight ounce can of tomato sauce
- one teaspoon of dried oregano

Directions:

Preheat oven to 350 degrees Fahrenheit. Spiralize your potatoes into spaghetti size noodles. Stir in butter, egg, and Parmesan. Coat a nine inch pie plate with cooking spray. Then, take the potato mixture and press it onto the bottom and sides of the pie plate to form a crust. In a skillet heat oil over medium heat adding sausage, onion, bell pepper, and garlic cooking for several minutes. Drain. Stir in tomato sauce and oregano and heat through. Spread the cottage cheese over the top of the potato pie crust. Spread meat mixture over cottage cheese then top with shredded mozzarella. Bake for 25 minutes or until it is baked through. Let it cool for five minutes then serve.

Chapter 6:
Spiralized Fish & Seafood Main Dishes

Something that my family loves is seafood so if you and your family love them too you will enjoy these wonderful spiralized fish and seafood dishes offered in this chapter. This food group is great source of omega-3's also known as brain food!

28. Lime-Garlic Shrimp with Spinach & Zucchini Noodles

Serves: 2 (just double up on ingredients to make enough for 4 servings)

Ingredients:

- 15 large shrimp, peeled and deveined
- two zucchini, spiralized
- half a teaspoon of coconut oil, melted
- one tablespoon of fresh parsley, minced
- zest from half a lime
- lime juice from half a lime
- one tablespoon of organic butter
- one cup of baby spinach
- sea salt
- black pepper

Directions:

In a bowl combine oil, garlic, lime juice, lime zest, salt and pepper. Let sit for 30 minutes. Spiralize your zucchini into spaghetti size noodles. Set aside. Heat up butter over medium heat. Add shrimp with marinade. Cook for 30 seconds. Remove shrimp with slotted spoon from pan and set aside. Add your zucchini noodles to the pan and toss lightly for two minutes. Add spinach, shrimp to pan with zucchini. Add salt and pepper to taste and squeeze juice from remaining half of lime into it.

29. Shrimp & Scallops with Butternut Squash

Serves: 6
Ingredients:

- two large butternut squash necks, spiralized
- four tablespoons of coconut oil, melted
- one pound of jumbo shrimp, peeled, and deveined
- one pound of scallops
- one tablespoon of garlic, minced
- one red onion, chopped
- 28- ounce can of diced tomatoes
- quarter teaspoon of paprika
- three turkey sausage, thickly sliced
- one teaspoon of black pepper
- half a cup of low-sodium chicken broth
- six tablespoons of fresh parsley, chopped
- lime wedges for garnish (optional)

Directions:

Spiralize your butternut squash into spaghetti size noodles. Set aside. In skillet heat three tablespoons of oil and add shrimp on medium heat. Cook for five minutes turn once. Transfer shrimp to a plate. Add scallops to skillet and sear for half a minute on each side. Transfer to plate with shrimp. Add turkey sausage slices to the pan cook for three minutes. Add remaining one tablespoon of oil, garlic, tomatoes, salt, paprika, pepper, saute for several minutes. Add chicken broth to skillet reduce the heat to medium. Stir in the squash noodles and simmer for several minutes. Add shrimp and scallops to the mixture in skillet. Add to serving dish and garnish with fresh parsley. Serve and enjoy!

30. Tuna & Zucchini Casserole

Serves: 4
Ingredients:

- two zucchini, spiralize one zucchini, and cut the other into one quarter- inch slices
- one celery stalk, chopped
- one teaspoon of garlic, minced
- two teaspoons of extra virgin olive oil, divided
- 2- 5 ounce cans of tuna, drained and flaked
- half a cup of mayonnaise
- half a cup of low-fat sour cream
- two tablespoons of Dijon mustard
- half a teaspoon of dried Thyme
- one quarter teaspoon of black pepper
- one cup of Monterey Jack cheese, shredded
- two tablespoons of fresh basil, chopped
- three green onions, thinly sliced

Directions:

Preheat oven to 375 degrees Fahrenheit. Spiralize one zucchini into spaghetti size noodles set in paper towel lined bowel. Set aside. In a large skillet saute zucchini slices in a teaspoon of oil until crispy. Remove from skillet. Saute celery in the remaining oil until crispy. Add garlic and saute for a minute or so. In large bowl add tuna, sour cream, green onions, thyme, salt, pepper, mayonnaise, and mustard and celery. Mix well. Add spiralized zucchini and toss to combine. In a greased 11×7 baking dish; add half of zucchini noodle mixture. Then, top with zucchini slices and repeat layers. Cook at 375 degrees Fahrenheit for 30 minutes. Sprinkle basil over to of casserole and serve.

31. Salmon & Creamy Dill Sauce with Zucchini Noodles

Serves: 4
Ingredients:

- two zucchini, spiralized
- one pound of fresh salmon, cut into four evenly sized pieces
- pinch of sea salt
- pinch of black pepper
- one serving cup of Greek plain yogurt
- one tablespoon of fresh dill weed
- half a teaspoon of grated lemon zest
- one tablespoon of lemon juice
- one tablespoon of coconut oil, melted

Directions:

Preheat oven 375 degrees Fahrenheit. Place your salmon in a large baking dish with the skin side facing down. Brush with olive oil over salmon. Season with salt and pepper. Bake for 25 minutes. Spiralize zucchini into fettuccine size noodles. When the salmon is almost done place your noodles in the boiling water for two minutes then remove. In skillet add oil on medium heat add the zucchini noodles and saute for a few minutes or until noodles become tender. In bowl mix yogurt, dill, lemon zest, lemon juice, and pepper. Mix well. Place zucchini noodles onto serving plate then add some dill sauce. Add your salmon on top and add more dill sauce on top of salmon.

32. Tilapia & Dijon Cream Sauce with Pasta

Serves: 2
Ingredients:

- two tilapia filets
- two zucchini, spiralized
- pinch of sea salt
- one lime, halved
- three quarter of a cup of low-sodium chicken broth
- three tablespoons of Dijon mustard
- one teaspoon of cilantro
- two tablespoons of light whipping cream
- one teaspoon of ground cumin

Directions:

Preheat the oven to 375 degrees Fahrenheit. Spiralize your zucchini into fettuccine size noodles. Set into bowl lined with paper towel and set aside. Spray a baking sheet with cooking spray then place your tilapia fillets on it. Lightly squeeze some fresh squeezed lime juice over your filets. Season with salt and pepper. Bake fish for 15 minutes or until it is cooked through.

In a frying pan add cilantro, mustard, chicken broth, and cumin. Whisk these ingredients around mixing them well, add your zucchini noodles and whipping cream simmer for two minutes or until heated through. Remove your zucchini noodles leaving sauce still in the pan with utensil that is porous. Transfer the noodles to serving plates. Top with the tilapia, and pour cream sauce over the top and serve.

33. Spicy Shrimp & Parsnip Noodles

Serves: 4
Ingredients:

- one pound of shrimp, peeled, and deveined
- three parsnips, spiralized
- one tablespoon of fresh parsley, chopped
- sea salt and pepper to taste
- half a teaspoon of chili powder
- one teaspoon of garlic, minced
- one quarter of a teaspoon of red pepper flakes
- half a cup of low-sodium chicken broth
- three tablespoons of coconut oil, melted
- one cup of red onion, diced

Directions:

Spiralize your parsnips into wide egg noodle style noodles. Set aside in a bowl lined with paper towel. In a skillet heat to medium heat two tablespoons of coconut oil, add onion and saute for five minutes. Add the garlic and the red pepper flakes sauteing for an additional two minutes. Add the remaining one tablespoon of oil to skillet along with your parsnip noodles. Add salt, pepper, chili powder.

Cook for five minutes or until your noodles are softened. Move your noodles to the side of your skillet then add the chicken broth and shrimp. Cook the shrimp for two minutes then turn shrimp over to cook the other side for two more minutes. Gently toss the shrimp and noodles together. Remove from heat and put into serving bowls add fresh parsley as a garnish if you wish and enjoy!

34. Crab & Kohlrabi Noodles

Serves: 4
Ingredients:

- two kohlrabi, spiralized
- one large package of frozen crab pieces
- two tablespoons of organic butter
- two tablespoons of coconut oil, melted
- half a cup of dry white wine
- two tablespoons of lemon juice
- half a cup of fresh parsley, chopped
- sea salt
- black pepper, freshly ground
- Parmesan cheese, shredded
- one cup of asparagus, cut diagonally into three inch pieces

Directions:

Allow your package of crab meat to defrost. Once crab meat is defrosted slice it up into smaller pieces or shred. Spiralize your kohlrabi into spaghetti size noodles. Put your noodles into a bowl lined with paper towel and set aside. In a skillet heat up your butter and oil over medium heat. Add the garlic and saute. Add lemon juice and wine and simmer for ten minutes. Add the asparagus and your kohlrabi noodles cover the skillet for five minutes to steam. Allow asparagus to become tender-crisp and your kohlrabi soft. Add your pieces of crab meat and toss lightly. Add salt and pepper, top with parsley and parmesan once in serving bowls.

35. Grilled Shrimp & Lime Basil Dressing with Zucchini Noodles

Serves: 4
Ingredients:

- one shallot, chopped
- one tablespoon of red wine vinegar
- one teaspoon of garlic, minced
- two cups of fresh basil, chopped
- one third cup of slivered almonds, divided
- half a cup of coconut oil, melted
- one tablespoon of extra virgin olive oil
- one pound of shrimp, peeled and deveined
- three zucchini, spiralized
- salt and pepper to taste
- four tablespoons of lemon basil dressing

Directions:

In a blender combine lime zest, half of your almonds, basil, shallot, garlic, red pepper flakes, extra virgin olive oil, and red wine vinegar. Blend until these ingredients are smooth. Season with salt and pepper then set aside. Heat a tablespoon of coconut oil over medium heat adding shrimp. Cook your shrimp for four minutes or until fully cooked. Remove shrimp from heat. Mix in two tablespoons of lemon basil dressing. Transfer your shrimp to a serving bowl using slotted spoon and set aside. Spiralize zucchini into spaghetti size noodles add them to the same pan you used for your shrimp and saute noodles for two minutes. Add two remaining tablespoons of lemon basil dressing toss to coat then remove from heat. Place noodles on serving dishes then put the shrimp on top of noodles season with salt, fresh ground pepper and remaining slivered almonds. Enjoy!

Chapter 7:
Spiralized Vegetarian Main Dishes

Here are some great tasting spiralized vegetarian recipes that you and your family are sure to enjoy. It is a healthy way to cut back on meats or if you are just trying to add a different approach to the family meal. It can be fun and exciting getting away from the regular meals and serving your family a new dish that is healthy, quick and easy to prepare.

36. Sauteed Mushrooms & Baby Spinach with Squash Noodles

Serves: 4
Ingredients:

- two sweet potato squash, spiralized
- five ounces of mushrooms, sliced
- eight ounces of baby spinach
- half a cup of low-sodium chicken broth
- one teaspoon of garlic, minced
- one leek, thinly sliced
- four tablespoons of coconut oil, melted
- half a cup of dry white wine
- salt and pepper
- two green onions, chopped
- two tablespoons of fresh parsley, chopped

Directions:

Spiralize your sweet potato squash into spaghetti size noodles. Place in a bowl lined with paper towel and set aside. In a frying pan saute your leek and garlic for two minutes in oil. Add mushrooms and continue to saute until mushrooms become browned. Add your spinach to the pan and pour in the chicken broth and wine. Add salt and pepper. Stir in your noodles and saute for a few more minutes tossing lightly. Remove from heat and serve right away.

37. Butternut Squash & Roasted Sweet Potato with Zucchini Pasta

Serves: 4
Ingredients:

- one butternut squash, peeled
- two sweet potatoes, spiralized
- two zucchini, spiralized
- one cup of asparagus, cut into three inch lengths
- half a cup of Monterey Jack cheese
- one third cup of dry white wine
- sea salt and pepper to taste

Directions:

Preheat your oven to 375 degrees Fahrenheit. Spiralize your zucchini into spaghetti size noodles. Put into a bowl lined with paper towel and set aside. Spiralize your sweet potato and neck of butternut squash into spaghetti size noodles. Remove the seeds from the bulb of your squash and chop into cubes about an inch in size. Place your asparagus and butternut cubes on a baking sheet and drizzle with oil tossing to coat. Sprinkle with salt and pepper. Roast for 25 minutes or until they are tender and crispy. In a skillet add two tablespoons of coconut oil over medium heat adding sweet potato and squash noodles. Saute your noodles for about four minutes or until they are beginning to soften. Add the cheese, wine, and zucchini noodles into pan and toss to coat. Cook for about another two minutes or until the cheese has melted. Remove from heat. Add your roasted butternut squash and asparagus to the top of noodles after they have been put on serving plates and enjoy!

38. Anchovies & Roasted Garlic Tomatoes with Butternut Squash Noodles

Serves: 4
Ingredients:

- two anchovy fillets packed in oil
- one quarter cup of organic butter
- one teaspoon of garlic, minced
- 1-28- ounce can of crushed tomatoes
- one butternut squash, spiralized
- Parmesan cheese, finely grated for garnish
- freshly ground black pepper
- sea salt
- half a teaspoon of red pepper flakes
- half a cup of white onion, finely sliced
- half cup of vegetable broth

Directions:

Preheat oven to 375 degrees Fahrenheit. Combine tomatoes, anchovies, garlic, butter, red pepper flakes on a 13×9 inch baking sheet. Season with salt and pepper. Roast this tomato mix in the oven for 40 minutes. Gently toss the mixture halfway through the cooking process. Add the mixture and vegetable broth to large sauce pan. Spiralize your butternut squash into fettuccine size noodles then add to pan with tomato sauce mixture.

Cook over medium heat for seven minutes. Top with Parmesan cheese and serve.

39. Butternut Squash & Rosemary Sauce with Zucchini Noodles

Servings: 4
Ingredients:

- one butternut squash
- one tablespoon of garlic, minced
- one cup of half-and-half whipping cream
- pinch of dried rosemary
- three tablespoons of coconut oil, melted, divided
- one white onion, chopped
- half a cup of low-sodium chicken broth
- fourteen ounces of portabella mushrooms, sliced
- two green onions, chopped
- four zucchini, spiralized
- fresh ground black pepper
- sea salt to taste

Directions:

Preheat oven to 425 degrees Fahrenheit. Slice your butternut squash in half lengthwise and remove the seeds. Place the cut side down of squash onto the baking sheet and cover with tin foil. Roast squash for about 45 minutes or until the squash is tender. Cool squash. When your squash has cooled scoop out and add to blender. In a small pan heat one tablespoon of coconut oil over medium heat. Add onions and garlic and saute for three minutes.

Add the onions, garlic, rosemary, chicken broth, whipping cream to the blender with the squash. Blend until smooth. Add the remaining coconut oil to large pan and saute the mushrooms for about five minutes. Spiralize your zucchini into fettuccine size noodles. Add these noodles to the mushrooms and saute for three minutes. Add the sauce to the pan and continue to cook for another three minutes or until sauce is hot. Put into serving bowls and garnish with chopped green onions and black pepper.

40. Avocado, Carrot, Feta Wrap with Zucchini Noodles

Servings: for 1 Wrap
Ingredients:

- three tablespoons of feta cheese, crumbled
- two tablespoons of hummus
- one tortilla whole wheat wrap
- one small carrot, spiralized
- half a zucchini, spiralized
- one quarter cup of chick peas, drained and rinsed
- one quarter avocado, sliced
- fresh ground black pepper to taste

Directions:

Take your tortilla and spread the hummus evenly over it. Add avocado. Season with pepper. Spiralize carrot, and zucchini into spaghetti size noodles. Place carrots and zucchini noodles into wrap cover with chick peas. Add feta cheese to top. Roll up and secure with toothpicks. You can make two smaller wraps by slicing it in half. This makes a great meal when you are on the go and need something healthy and quick!

Conclusion

I hope that you and your family will enjoy making these healthy fun, spiralized recipes for many years to come. It can be very challenging in the world today to try and find foods that your whole family will enjoy. Sometimes when you approach the way you present foods to them by using spiralizing them for example it can truly draw their attention to the meals being put in front of them in a new refreshed outlook. Healthy foods do not have to be boring the recipes in this book will most certainly prove that! Best of luck to cooking your way to a life full of optimal health and wellness!

Finally, if you enjoyed this book, then I'd like to ask you for a big favor, would you be kind enough to leave a review for this book on Amazon? It'd be greatly appreciated! I wish you the best of luck and enjoy your new healthy Spiralized recipes!

Eric Deen

Free Bonus

As my way of saying thank you for reading this book, I've included a very special gift for you; I want to give you a complete e-book called "Weight Loss Enigma".

With this great eBook you'll discover:

- How to lose weight successfully by understanding what the breaking down of food is like within our body...
- Why using food diary could help you to lose weight...
- Identifying your Health and Weight Profile for Successful Weight Loss...
- How to get into shape by exercise that do not required you to visit to the gym?
- Find out the eight most handful tips and effective method in losing weight...
- And much more...

With this special gift you will learn the secret of how to effectively shedding off the excessive bulging belly & stay a healthy shape in no time!

Copy the link below in your browser. My friend David Smith (who is my publisher) will send you the eBook to your email.

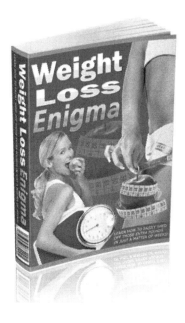

Link:

http://bit.ly/1AhFYqk

DISCLAIMER AND/OR LEGAL NOTICES: Every effort has been made to accurately represent this book and it's potential. Results vary with every individual, and your results may or may not be different from those depicted. No promises, guarantees or warranties, whether stated or implied, have been made that you will produce any specific result from this book. Your efforts are individual and unique, and may vary from those shown. Your success depends on your efforts, background and motivation.

The material in this publication is provided for educational and informational purposes only and is not intended as medical advice. The information contained in this book should not be used to diagnose or treat any illness, metabolic disorder, disease or health problem. Always consult your physician or health care provider before beginning any nutrition or exercise program. Use of the programs, advice, and information contained in this book is at the sole choice and risk of the reader.

Made in the USA
Middletown, DE
18 October 2015